BULLETPROOF
RETIREMENT

LIVE YOUR DREAMS, AVOID EXCESS FEES,
AND SECURE YOUR LEGACY

MARTIN WILCOCKS

Dear James,

It's a far cry from our days at the bank. Hope you enjoy my book and it paves the way for a continuous recurring support with the mission. Best

Martin

R^ethink

First published in Great Britain in 2022
by Rethink Press (www.rethinkpress.com)

Disclaimer

The views expressed in this book do not constitute financial
advice. The investment ideas discussed should never be
used without first assessing your own financial situation and
consulting a qualified financial adviser. Neither the author
nor the publisher can be held responsible for any losses that
may result from investments made after reading this book.

I dedicate this book to my family, all of whom are sacred
and have helped me in one way or another to be me
Martin, Gareth and Alan, all rolled into one

Contents

.

Introduction

What would you like to do when you retire? Take that dream holiday, buy a yacht and sail around the world? Or perhaps you'd like to keep it simple: enjoy your garden and new hobbies, volunteer in the community, look after your grandchildren? You might even have a plan for a new business venture or project. Alternatively, you may be thinking 'retirement – what retirement?' Even for people in their 50s, retirement might seem way too far off to worry about today.

Your attitude to retirement will depend on three things: your age, your state of health and your life-long approach to pensions, savings and financial risk. However, there's a bigger question I'd like you to think about. What impact and influence do you want to have – on the world, in your family, within your community and on the environment?

Many people find it hard to talk about their personal finances openly; it is an emotive subject for them. When thinking about their future, they don't know who to trust or where to turn. They don't know the right questions to ask to get the advice that they need. They don't even know what they don't know.

And unfortunately, for reasons that I will explain in *Bulletproof Retirement*, even people who have paid good money for financial advice can approach retirement with:

- No plan for their future at all

- Plans that have substandard and costly investments behind them

- No basic tax allowances used to enhance their plan

- No provision for their family, who could be left destitute on premature death or illness

- No tax-efficient succession plan to pass the 'family pot' on safely

Many retirement plans are also hamstrung by what I have identified as the £64 billion problem that stands in the way of the average customer, seeking to plan their retirement and leave a legacy for loved ones or charity. In Chapter Two I show how British people pay £64 billion annually to financial institutions in unnecessary costs and fees for investment management, and this could be reinvested into your retirement plan. It's a problem that repeats itself every year, and it means you risk making huge financial mistakes that you'll regret in your retirement years. It's the financial scandal nobody's talking about and yet it's perfectly legal. Around 2,000 people retire in the UK every day, and this affects their ability to be financially viable and comfortable in later life.[1]

In the first part of *Bulletproof Retirement*, I will outline how I have reached this conclusion. My analysis is mainly based on the practices of certain financial networks (I talk about the 'glossy networks' a lot in this book) and financial advisers whose focus is on feathering the nests of the institutions they work for, rather than that of the customer (you). You'll discover how the excess fees that many networks and advisers charge are crippling people's retirement plans.

My goal for three decades has been to listen to ordinary people and help them achieve the retirement they want. I set up my own business as an independent financial adviser fourteen years ago, but I started in Barclays Bank in 1989. I first found my niche as a personal banker, then became a financial adviser with Barclays Life, then returned to the bank as a premier manager. Finally, I spent three years as a restricted adviser operating under a large network. I thought I had found a home for life, but the organisation was too complex, too expensive, with too many chiefs. I was restricted in my ability to advise independently and had to sell the network's funds. So, by the time I set up on my own in 2006, I had witnessed all the problems with the creation and protection of wealth in the UK.

The global financial crash of 2008 hit me hard two years into my own operation, by which time my brother Rob had joined me. I had a young family and had taken out a big mortgage. This is the back story that has shaped my own business and explains why I put customers first and always will. Anything other than prioritising the customers' needs is unacceptable and a business that fails to do this won't earn their support.

Good independent financial advisers are like a compass in your pocket: they can help you plan for your future and offer you a clear and navigable path towards reaching your goals. They will help you execute your plan while keeping you sane when the markets implode, as they do on a regular basis. And I will explain in *Bulletproof Retirement* that you'll need to be in the markets because you need to invest in equities; nothing else will provide real growth.

The problem is that people are scared of the markets, especially when they can see them going into free fall, as they did most recently in the first quarter of 2020 due to the global COVID-19 crisis. The worst factor for the markets, and for all of us watching them, was uncertainty; we had no idea how long the pandemic would last (a lot longer than many of us probably expected, as it turned out) and what the economic impact would be (considerable). We know that, even when the pandemic is under control, something else, somewhere in the world, will affect the markets.

We can't control what happens to the markets, but we can control how we behave in response. You will see from the following chapters that my advice will always be to stay calm, take the long view and watch the highs and lows even out over time. Most of the time, markets that fall quickly bounce back and rise, but by then people have panicked and thrown their pensions, individual savings accounts (ISAs) or general investment accounts overboard. The damage is usually irreparable. So, I will explain why we need to focus on equities and demonstrate why the future doesn't rest in fixed income investments. As the great US adviser Nick Murray says, signing up for a fixed-income retirement in a rising-cost world is a financial suicide plan in instalments.[2]

In the first part of *Bulletproof Retirement*, I will break down the £64 billion problem and some of the common but unworkable retirement plans and suggest a more viable path. In short, we need to plan for our retirement sooner, and plan better, following a proper process.

My other purpose in writing *Bulletproof Retirement* is to raise awareness that there *are* advisers who follow financial planning models that work in the real interests of their clients, who put their clients first and want to work with them in the long term. That requires calling attention to the good independent financial advisers who run their own, perhaps smaller, practices. In particular, it means understanding that big (as in the banks and glossy networks) is no guarantee of better, and that a small practice is governed by *slightly* different, equally stringent regulations that the Financial Conduct Authority (FCA) sets down.

My own business currently looks after 115 families and 170 individual investors, and typically takes on a new family every month. The firm's plan has always been to make a difference to 500 families. If every decent financial planning adviser could do that for 500 families, collectively we would make a massive difference to the creation and protection of wealth in the UK.

My goal in this book is to help people understand the cost of their ideal lifestyle, and maintain it through the likely three-decade retirement most can expect without running out of money. They need to know that their financial adviser's plan follows a proper process and has a trusty investment engine behind it. They need to utilise all available tax allowances, steer clear of ridiculous tax avoidance schemes and the questionable advice behind them, get a grip on the likely effect of a catastrophe such as premature death or illness on their business (if they have one) and, crucially, on the family unit. We help our clients put a protective platform in place to look after partners and dependent children, before carving out a plan to pass their 'pot' on safely and tax-efficiently.

In the second part of *Bulletproof Retirement*, therefore, I outline my CLEARER™ model, the fruits of my three decades' experience in finance, that my firm developed to help our clients make these important decisions. I will share the stories of those who have been in circumstances similar to yours and have had similar concerns about their future. I've been privileged to help them plan for their future retirements and I'm proud that, in many cases, my efforts have helped transform their lives.

I'd like this book to play its part in teaching something that isn't taught in schools: to understand how money works. So many fundamental mistakes in financial planning for retirement can be avoided with basic knowledge.

I hope that *Bulletproof Retirement* will encourage you to begin, or review, your own retirement plans with confidence, in the knowledge that you can look forward to your future life without worry. I can help steer you through the fog, walking you through the CLEARER™ model, supported with online resources that will help you ask yourself the right questions, give you a game plan to achieve your heart's desire and help you get the in-depth advice you need.

First, let's talk about your dream retirement.

PART ONE

WHAT IS RETIREMENT?

1

Retirement Nowadays

We are all living longer, with bigger dreams and hopes than ever before. We might think we all know what retirement means, but how many of us have actually given it the serious thought it deserves?

My dad is typical of his generation, a child of the Second World War era born out of the Great Depression. He was a detective in the CID and retired in his late 50s, after almost thirty years' service. For him and my grandparents before him, retirement (for men at least) was when people stopped working at their full-time job and hung their boots up.

A couple's expectations upon retirement were shared; they'd worked, put aside some savings (if they could), they'd paid their 'stamp' and could look forward to collecting their old age pension. Most men stopped work at 65, women at 60. They then lived out their remaining ten to fifteen years drawing on their savings and being looked after financially by the state.

Retirement as our parents knew it, in the 'good old days', dates from a time when many people worked just for one company, or in one industry, usually for decades, after which they might or might not receive a pension; if they did, it was enough to live on for the relatively short lifespan after retirement. Mr and Mrs Average live longer today. The following numbers, provided by the Resolution think-tank in 2017,[3] ask us to re-evaluate retirement.

- By 2040 nearly one in seven Britons will be over 75.

- Almost a third of people born today can expect to live until they are 100.

- In 2014, the average age in the UK was above 40 for the first time.

- In 2017, the ratio of non-workers to workers started to rise for the first time since the early 1980s.

Back in 1972, when I was born, it was generally expected that anyone of the postwar generation retiring at 65 would live for another ten or fifteen years and that anyone older than 80 was exceptional. In the twenty-first century, however, thanks to medical advances, higher living standards, better diets and so forth, we can expect to live into our late 80s and many will live into our early 90s. Reaching three figures is no longer unusual. How does anyone expect their savings to carry them through this extended retirement?

Also, we now expect to live life more fully outside an active working life. A 60-year-old in the 1960s looked, acted and sounded much older than a 60-year-old today. I have a client, Mary, who is a great traveller, fulfilling lifelong dreams in her retirement by visiting exotic locations such as Machu Picchu. Mary typifies many active retirees I know who were born in the 'baby boom' (between 1943 and 1965). They are making the most of their time, unlike my grandmother who, in her 60s, sought pleasure in two packets of Players No 6 whilst doing the pools and catching up on *Crossroads*. The younger baby boomers are retiring now at the rate of 2,000 a day. However, the generous pension pots of old aren't so readily available any more and, coupled with the huge increase in personal debt for some, this may mean that retirement today can be drastically delayed, or even (for some) remain a pipe dream. Against that background of changing expectations, challenges and opportunities presented by a longer, healthier old age, what role does the wider financial industry play in our retirement plans?

The way we approach finance, and the framework within which we all work, earn, spend and save is, in my opinion, flawed. My thirty years spent working in the financial industry, together with the research I have undertaken (specifically on the last of the baby boomers, who are due to retire within the next ten years) paints a gloomy picture.

Working against us is the £64 billion problem in the financial industry, which I will explain in more detail in Chapter Two. For those who are approaching retirement blissfully unaware that this has anything to do with them, and who even think they have plans in place, it's going to hurt.

As I said in the Introduction, most people are not comfortable discussing money, and the result can be that they drift through life with no financial plan. Those that do have a plan sometimes learn they've been let down by advisers who don't have their best interests at heart. They may have found that the 'investment managers' who were supposed to be looking after their money were, in reality, just overpaid fund or stock pickers and market traders.

Unfortunately, too many people who think they have plans simply discover too late that those plans are not worth the paper they're written on. And in many cases, they end up dependent financially on their children, and on the state. I'm out to put a stop to all of that.

This fundamental £64 billion flaw in the system has not changed, despite media spotlights on the financial markets and several government reviews of financial services in recent years. As the last of the baby boomers reach retirement, they're in a vulnerable position when it comes to their savings and future financial health. That begs the question, what are their options?

- Does retirement become a challenge, something to fear, something to dread?

- Does retirement even disappear in a puff of smoke?

- Or does retirement open up new opportunities that can be funded?

The good news is that I have developed with my clients a more lasting and satisfying process of planning for your retirement. Below are just a few of the questions I ask clients, to build a full picture of what they want and need in the future. (My CLEARER™ model, outlined in Part Four, describes my process in more depth.) If anyone claims to be giving you financial advice, these are the questions they should be asking you, so thinking about these points yourself is a good preparation for conversations with advisers.

- How will you pay for the future lifestyle you want? One that you can look forward to now and then live it with complete pleasure and certainty?

- What does this lifestyle look like? Who will be living it with you?

- What is most important to your happiness (holidays, special-occasion treats, hobbies, other activities)? What do you need to set aside for these purposes?

- Do you want to continue to enjoy the lifestyle you enjoy now? Is there something you don't do now, but would like to take up?

- Have you got a strategy for making sure your income continues to cover your lifestyle throughout a three-decade retirement?

- Who will receive your estate?

It used to be simple to save for your retirement. Besides stuffing cash under the mattress, people deposited sums in a bank or building society, or possibly bought stocks and shares. The more adventurous would try a managed investment fund. The money would be ready to be drawn down in retirement. Even today, this is how some people still save and manage their money.

However, there are three problems with the old, simple approach.

- Leaving it in simple bank deposits will see it eaten away by inflation. In my experience, people doing this never have a viable, futureproof financial plan.

- Many standard (ie unreviewed) managed investment plans don't even keep pace with the benchmark index they track. More on this in Chapter Seven.

- It's not always clear nowadays who people can trust in the financial world, especially after the global financial crash and various mis-selling controversies.

We all need to think differently about saving, to feel able to trust the people who support us in making financial decisions and to understand better how we can invest. We also need to address the other great myth in personal finance, the myth of risk. I can remember vividly a day in my childhood when my parents sat in the kitchen, earnestly discussing their savings. They had spent a while shopping around for the best rate for a 12-month cash account. The differential they were discussing was 0.2%. Inflation was over 6% at that time. To their credit, at least they were discussing it and shopping around. The far bigger issue was their approach to risk. They had limited their own choices because they were risk-averse.

The myth of risk

Conversations about risk are hard. Talking to clients about risk can feel like sticking pins in them to see how much pain they can absorb. Quite often an individual's approach to risk is a result of their level of education, or lack of it, about financial matters. I've known clients who feel very uncomfortable if their investments drop at any point. A few will even panic. Their lack of knowledge about risk leads them to believe that the risk arises when investments go down

– in fact, that's a good example of confusing price gyration, the natural ebb and flow of the markets, with risk. Price gyration is not the same as volatility (a term scary enough in its own right). I will explain in Chapter Two.

The fact is, prices go up and down. That's nothing to be worried about. In order for your money to outlive you, you need to accept a certain amount of movement in your investments. Part of my purpose in writing this book is to help you navigate the opaque world of finance, giving you as much clarity as I can.

The more we can all distinguish between what is necessary and what is a pitfall, the better our financial planning decisions will be. That requires us to shift our view of what retirement means. The very notion of retirement means different things to different people: slowing down, part-time consulting for a few days per week, or just finishing our working days with hopefully many years ahead to look forward to. But to do what? Buy that yacht? Take those holidays? Splash out on those landmark special occasions? Immerse ourselves in community work? Strive to make a difference? Leave a legacy?

We need to be able to fund whatever we want to do in our later years. The financial system may be broken, but none of us should accept that as limiting our dreams for retirement. So, creating the right financial plan for your retirement becomes more and more important, but it can also feel like navigating through a minefield. Do you choose an independent adviser, or a restricted adviser? And what is the difference? Maybe you decide to lean on the government for help and contact their dedicated pensions advice centre. Alas, there is not a great deal this quango can actually do. They can't advise you what to do, or what you need. Instead, they have to send you to a regulated adviser – so you're back to the independent or restricted choice.

How do you choose an adviser? Do you pick the network that gives you the impression they are the best and strongest option? They may remind you that they are listed on the London (or Frankfurt, or New York) Stock Exchange and that their advice is guaranteed. You may note they have battalions of advisers, and those advisers' managers, and then some local directors, and area directors, and other chiefs. And then there's a fleet of flagship offices in high-end locations, a board and a committee. Who pays for all this, you may ask? Good question.

Or do you choose a smaller, family firm? It is governed and regulated by the FCA (just as the big firms are), with the advice it gives also governed by the same rules, and if anything goes wrong the Financial Services Compensation Scheme (FSCS) can step in, just as it would if a big firm went under. It will have its own professional indemnity cover, but above all else it depends much more directly on keeping its customer happy – you.

Pro rata, independent advisers that are not attached to a network pay exactly the same taxes and levies per transaction, per customer, and the licence terms are just as stringent. We operate under the same rules, but we are very different.

You may feel a bit like a ship at sea minus a compass, unsure of whom to trust, and where to turn. My priority is always to understand what a client wants to achieve with their life. The fact is, financial products have no meaning unless they can help you fulfil life goals. What's the money for, after all? While every person is unique, with different needs, and while there's no such thing as a one-size-fits-all approach, the reality is that most people want similar things (such as better returns), so they will have more time to enjoy life generally, and most of the time that involves spending time with loved ones, travelling, short breaks and holidays and providing support for children, or other things close to the heart.

I don't recall ever meeting anybody who wasn't dreaming of *a comfortable retirement* that was set up to allow them to do all the things they ever wanted without worrying about running short, or even out, of money. These dreams are what life is all about.

Then there is the ability to make *an impact in the life of children*, or indeed grandchildren, perhaps by supporting education costs, or providing time rather than money. Some have one eye on the children, and the other eye on aging parents of their own, who may be in their later years and not quite as agile as they once were. Family is sacred.

The other key consideration is *the ultimate passage* for all the hard-earned money and other wealth. Who does it end up with, and will it get there safely and tax-efficiently? Should it be inherited directly, or is the estate quite large (always subjective)? If so, would its size create other potential issues and put our beneficiaries in a vulnerable position? Perhaps there's a need to pass assets in a controlled way and minus a flogging from HMRC, who continue to strip estates of billions every year in unplanned inheritance tax. Legacy is how you live on and have an impact on your bloodline for perhaps the next century, after you pass.

Every customer I have met and advised for the past thirty years had at least one of those three overall needs. Most have two. Around half have all three.

Trust and confidence are key in what I deliver, and these areas of planning underpin the relationship I have with a client; once they know their best interests are at the heart of the conversation, the trust I refer to builds. It can't be bought on day one, so people have to give the relationship with an adviser a go based on assumptions and their gut feelings. That trust is absolutely crucial when the market tanks, which it does every seven years or so. You need a solid relationship with an adviser who you can speak with personally and professionally. A good adviser is your financial planner, investment and asset manager, and general counsel who you have engaged to help you make good decisions and help you avoid making bad ones.

The adviser's first task is to determine what the clients want to do in their retirement. Many respond to me with a selection of the following:

- Buy a yacht and sail around the world
- Work in the garden
- Volunteer in the community
- Pay for later-life care, if necessary
- Look after grandchildren
- Travel
- Take up an interest
- Spend more time playing tennis/golf/squash, or at the gym
- Set up a small business or project for love, not money

Most of the time, by 'legacy' we mean financial legacy: how much money and assets we leave behind. However, we should also think of legacy in much bigger terms, such as the relationships forged with friends, family and in our community. What would people say about you at your funeral? What difference, if any, might you have made to the world around you? Retirement, in that case, offers an opportunity beyond our careers and employment, to make a difference and to create a wider legacy.

Sadly, the flaws in the financial system place obstacles in your way as you try to achieve your dream retirement: notably the £64 billion that each year leaves the collective reserves of people planning for retirement and is paid over in excessive fees for highly priced investments, funds and advisers.

2
The 1.4% Challenge

The figure 1.4 sounds like a small number, doesn't it? It doesn't send us running for the hills. In fact, who's going to worry about handing over an extra 1.4% to a big-name, gilt-edged financial institution to run our future retirement affairs? After all, they're the experts, aren't they? If the experts are going to make us shed-loads of money by playing the markets with our investments, what's wrong (in the bigger scheme of things) in paying over an additional 1.4%?

In this chapter, I'll tell you how it began to dawn on me that the investment products I was selling back in the late 1990s and early 2000s were not always in the best interests of the customers. I'll also explain how that percentage differential translates into a number that will make your eyes water. If this has happened to you, you'll wonder how you ever agreed to it in the first place, but I'll show you how to prevent it happening again.

Every year, £64 billion (yes, your money, every year) is being creamed off your investments and I'm prepared to bet that many of you will never have noticed. If you have, and raised it with your adviser or fund manager, you have probably been talked back around, persuaded that the fees are justified.

This huge and staggering amount of money is being hived off by slick financial experts who rely on reminding you that they're the experts. Every now and then a financial portfolio statement might land on your doormat (or, if you've invested above a certain amount, be handed to you in person). If it's thick enough to have felled a forest, that's because your fund managers are very keen to show you how hard they've worked on your behalf. It's the tip of the iceberg and the biggest financial scandal in the UK, which nobody speaks about. That is, until now.

During the years I worked as an adviser with a major network, despite enjoying the freedom and ability to manage my own clients, I saw that its systems, processes and models were archaic, buried in a 1980s sales model to which expensive fees were woven in and remained hidden. The system of commission tiers, income generators and predictors made it almost impossible for me to calculate exactly how much income I was going to generate for myself. I was buried under layer upon layer of needless complexities with no room to breathe and no lights to guide me. It was like walking through a waist-high sea of mud.

When I eventually felt as though I was standing on something approaching solid ground, it then took another year or so to develop my clients. Only then did I feel more confident and focused on growing my client bank, but that sense of excitement didn't last. Before long, those same old nagging doubts that had bothered me at the end of my time at Barclays resurfaced, and I soon lacked any sense of purpose.

Again, I never felt that the customer's needs were the primary focus. My heart and my head kept telling me to look towards the customer but the network kept steering me towards its own investment funds and 'special' committee, which in my opinion was all gloss and no substance.

In 2006, all of this noise and nonsense created the driving force behind my leaving a, once again, well-paid (albeit self-employed) position with perks. I had decided by this stage to set up and run my own private practice where I could focus on my priority – customer-centred financial planning.

That was a bold move in that boom period; there weren't that many financial planners at that time who would stick their necks out, as I did, to help clients focus on the bigger picture, such as how much money they would need to sustain them comfortably through nearly three decades of retirement. I'd come to realise that nobody asked their clients, 'How much do you need?'

That's a vital question and there's no one-size-fits-all answer. My mission was to help clients understand their own unique set of circumstances and future needs by offering them sensible, fairly priced financial planning, which ultimately would put more money in their own pockets instead of lining those of the adviser. I knew that if I was fair with pricing I could make a good living and clients would have an incentive to stay with me for life. I played the long game.

As a one-man band, I would be regulated by the FCA in exactly the same way as the big investment banks and glossy networks. My customers would receive the same levels of financial protection from me as they would from anyone else but the big difference was that they also had my full attention. With the big networks and private banks they'd simply be a number on the receiving end of smooth talk and guarantees based on, for example, the firm's FTSE 100 status, plus billions of pounds of infrastructure and endless resources to throw at marketing. I'd already decided that in going it alone I could provide a better service for the customer, and it was better for my sanity.

The global financial crisis of 2008 landed in September 2007 for me: I was arranging a £1 million refinance for a house valued at £1.75 million, which should have been straightforward, but the lender pulled out. By the time the world collapsed in April 2008, we realised that there was no money left in the system. The timing couldn't have been worse but at least my principles were intact, despite the markets crashing all around me.

There was no way I would go running back to any of the big networks, although I certainly could have done because, fundamentally, nothing had really changed. Theirs was (and still is, to a large extent) a nepotistic system that's more often than not tied into selling their own highly priced products, or a selected number of 'third party' products, where the rewards are centred around bonuses. The network adviser's typical focus is on the products that carry the highest margins for them, not in offering truly independent advice based on the needs of the customer.

Independent operators, such as myself, however, will focus on what the investments will deliver for each tailored plan. This is quite a departure from where advisers in the big networks open their discussions with potential clients. Often, they are forced into the sales role from the outset, trying to sell products without any clear understanding of what those products are designed to do. They want the customer to sign up for an investment 'solution' that promises the earth and carries a cost that appears to be a small number, typically anything from around 2% at the lower end up to 3.5% at the higher end. The total cost is referred to as the OCF – ongoing charges figure. It's a collection of fees from the products, funds and services. Before the customers know it, they are bamboozled into paying out this money each year. Imagine what those numbers begin to look like once you learn that more than 80,000 people work in the fund management industry.[4]

My figure of £64 billion in unnecessary charges each year is based on industry research. The Investment Association's 2019 report showed that, of the £7.7 trillion invested in the UK in pensions, ISAs and general investments, 74% was actively managed. We know from a raft of other research that around 80% of actively managed money would have been better off in a low-cost passive investment:[5] these are described in Part Two, but can be likened to simply buying and holding a share in a mutual investment fund that invests in the Financial Times Stock Exchange (FTSE) 100 index. Warren Buffett supports this style of investing, as did the late John 'Jack' Bogle.[6][7]

I'll explain the methodology in more depth in Part Two, when we cover investing. For now, just accept that 80% of the 74% from that £7.7 trillion underperforms. That's £4.6 trillion every year paying higher, 'active' fees for sub-passive investment with inferior performance. I think paying around 1.6% per year for a great financial planning service that also takes care of your investments is a fair price. My findings show that actively managed investment services can see total fees charged at around double that. Let's say 3% on average; this means an extra 1.4% per year essentially on active management that doesn't deliver, in perhaps 80% of cases.

Table 1 *The 1.4%, 64 billion cost drag*

Funds Under Management as per IMA Report		£7.7 trillion
Actively Managed Element	74%	£5.7 trillion
Underperform Benchmark	80%	£4.6 trillion
Excess Costs	1.4%	£64 billion

With smaller independent advisers, such as myself, that 3% figure can be closer to 1.6%, a difference of approximately 1.4%. To be fair, there are advisers charging 1% and sometimes less than this, and I make no apology for my own fee tariff: it is what I think is fair for the services I provide.

I can also share real examples of active fees way in excess of 3%. Each year that 1.4% difference might seem small and inconsequential, but over a lifetime it could make the difference between taking that dream holiday, celebrating an important milestone, funding your care in old age or leaving a meaningful legacy, and being able to do none of those things. That is the reality of 1.4%.

In Part Two I'll explain in more detail why the big networks, investment houses and private banks may try to justify that extra 1.4% through their attempts to sell diversification via exposure to a small host of carefully selected funds. That approach is, in my experience, nonsensical because it's based on a subjective and scattergun approach and doesn't have the customer's long-term needs at heart. In contrast, I operate with a sense of purpose backed up by evidential research.

Having principles is one thing but knowing the facts and figures is just as vital and my chain of evidence stretches back to the 1950s. This evidence shows that equity markets in the developed world have more or less delivered a return of 10% per annum over the sixty-five years to 2020, averaged out over good and bad years. I say 'more or less' because multiplying together sixty-five individual, rounded, one-year returns can skew the results (depending on how many were rounded up, and how many down). That said, who wouldn't take 10% per year? But when the markets fall, as inevitably they do, the public are thrown into fear and panic by noise from the media, and many people sell their investments, tossing away their future.

Not always, but typically, an independent adviser leaning on evidence should tell you that it's better to invest into the global equity market, which could see your portfolio spread around 43,342 listed companies[8] (developed and emerging world) because doing so significantly reduces risk. When one equity fails, one of the other 43,341 may cover it.* In my mind, this is one of the major differences in approach between a network-based adviser and an independent adviser, where the advantage clearly rests with the customer.

Importantly, a passive global equity investment strategy may be less risky than an adviser's advice to perhaps hold a limited number of funds, or buy equities directly from stockbrokers or institutions. Whether the adviser and network are, or are not, a 'safe pair of hands', even if the current performance looks good, tomorrow that could change. Short-term good performance should not be used to hide from the investor the inherent risk in putting your eggs in a few baskets.

The truth is, the potential for loss of capital is huge if you only invest in a few funds, or in individual companies. Are you prepared to allow your money to be gambled through active investment management because such management has potential to deliver huge returns? The flip side is, of course, the real potential to deliver significant losses. You'll still be paying, whatever the outcome is.

The network-based stock and fund picking advisers may not tell you that 80% of their 'active management'

---

*   A large proportion of the current 43,342 are so small that it becomes impractical to own them in a portfolio due to trading costs and other risks that come with ownership. Many of these micro-caps will also be thinly traded, thus are susceptible to significant market impact if large trades take place.

doesn't deliver, with many fund managers failing to keep pace with whichever index they choose to benchmark themselves against (the FTSE 100, for instance). That's because they're trying to forecast the future and bet on it, and they don't always get it right.

Boring as it might sound, delivering financial and investment advice based on evidence, as I do, provides the customer with consistent results. Some customers might say this is too risk-averse and boring, but others see the attraction of a more reliable return that is more consistent, when it's presented to them in these terms.

One must tread carefully, as even passive investment can be full of traps set to extract needless sums of money from your pot. For example, while fees for passive management can appear low, it's easy to be lulled into a false sense of security when a respectable institution, or an adviser working for one, offers you a guarantee. Often, this is not a safety net, it's a trap. And this makes a big contribution to the annual £64 billion problem.

CASE STUDY: NEIL

Neil first contacted me in 2013 about his mother's estate. A year or so later he asked me to look at a pension fund worth £339,000.

He was nervous about risk and did not want his retirement fund to ever drop below that value, so he had invested his funds with a high street financial services company (not part of a glossy network; a sturdy, no-nonsense adviser). His total adviser fees per year amounted to 3.49%; in cash terms, an annual cost of £11,800.

Neil had always felt that he was serviced by little more than a glorified sales agent who didn't understand the rudiments of investing, or how to create a decent futureproof portfolio. As a result, his money was simply invested in a couple of standard managed funds. And he was paying a small fortune in fees.

Table 2 *Fees under Neil's old plan*

Charge	% of benefit base	Amount per annum
Trail commision	0.33	£1,107.58
Contract management	0.50	£1,678.15
Guarantee charge	1.85	£6,205.56

Fund Management Charges

- 0.50% p.a. for the Liquidity Fund
- 0.90% p.a. for UK Bond Fund
- 0.80% p.a. for Global Government Bond Fund
- 1.35% p.a. for Equity Funds
- 0.50% p.a. for Index Fund

The fee included a 'guarantee charge' of 1.85%. Some people like the word 'guarantee'. If I'm buying white goods from John Lewis, I'm happy to accept their five-year guarantee. After all, I don't apparently pay anything for it. Neil's guarantee wasn't free; and I don't believe he needed it anyway, as I will show below. His retirement funds were being needlessly reduced, I thought.

The average fund cost within Neil's plan was 0.81%, and when added to the trail commission his adviser was taking, pension provider contract costs and guarantee charge, the overall total cost (OCF) was 3.49% per annum.

When I took over managing Neil's fund, his overall fees reduced to 1.6%, an annual cost of £5,500, less than half the previous fee, and now bought him tailored financial planning and cash-flow projections as well as 'fund management'. As a result, he was able put £6,300 per annum back into his plan to support his income needs in retirement and his ultimate estate for his wife and their children.

If Neil lives to 94 (thirty years from when he retired), the effect of that £6,300 saving per year would be approximately £460,000 if his fund earned 5% per year (remember developed world markets have done twice that over the last seventy years). So why on earth was he paying that guarantee charge? He had been sold 'protection' that would put his risk-averse mind at ease. This protection was costing him approximately £7,000 per year. The only return Neil had was peace of mind, but at a very high price.

Nobody had explained to him the evidential history of the markets (that over seven decades, at least, any market fall has been temporary, but the rises have always been permanent). Incidentally, passive management of his funds seemed likely to return him more than the rather stodgy funds he had been sold.

As an example, the UK stock market has risen from 200 points to a high of 7,847 points during my lifetime (at least, between my birth in 1972 and when I started writing my book). I encouraged Neil to consider where the markets might be when he's 75 or 80, rather than looking at them in the short term.

He didn't need an 'insurance policy' that would protect his £339,000 but limit any growth he could earn by taking high fees out of the fund and choosing poor but 'safe' investments. When the markets did fall his provider could tell him, truthfully and with complete confidence, that he hadn't lost a penny. No one told Neil, however, that he was losing money through a flatlined investment and by paying over his annual fees every year.

His money was being dropped into that £64 billion per year pot of excess charges. It wasn't Black Monday (1987), Black Wednesday (1992), the 2008 financial crisis, COVID-19 or any major market fluctuation that placed Neil's money at risk, it was the institution he'd entrusted it to.

To avoid Neil's predicament, you have to take back control of your finances, and a little knowledge will give you the confidence to start to do that. Your journey towards a greater understanding of your finances begins now.

PART TWO

HOW MARKETS WORK

3

Main Types of Investment

Knowing a little about how the markets work and how they perform is invaluable before you seek any advice. You're trying to plan for thirty years or more beyond the moment you stop earning, so the better informed you are for that initial conversation with your adviser, the better armed you are.

Your adviser/financial planner/investment adviser is likely to assume that you understand what investing in the markets means. Financial terminology and jargon can be overwhelming and before you know it, you've submitted (through boredom, fear or plain exhaustion) and agreed to a plan of action that could potentially head in the wrong direction.

I hope this chapter will resolve any confusion and fear about how equity markets work. Since the industrial revolution, we've been unable to get by without investing in equities. Right now, with many people facing a potential three decades in retirement, we need them even more. The good news for us is that there is a world of opportunities in equities.

Equities

An equity market, no matter where it is, comprises a number of listed companies that are measured by market capitalisation (the value of the shares that shareholders have purchased). At the top end of the spectrum, the largest companies (like my former employer, Barclays) will list many hundreds of thousands of shares for the public to buy; these are known as 'large cap' stocks. Conversely, smaller companies – perhaps a Wilcocks & Wilcocks, if I was to float my firm on the market – may list fewer shares and would be classed as 'small cap'.

Each company's value is easy to measure by a simple calculation: multiplying the number of shares held by the share price. This gives us the 'market cap'. If we look at Barclays in December 2019, 17.35 billion shares were outstanding (issued and purchased) and with a price per share of just under £1 the market cap was £16.87 billion. A much smaller company may have 100 million shares outstanding at a price of £10 per share, resulting in a market cap of £1 billion – much

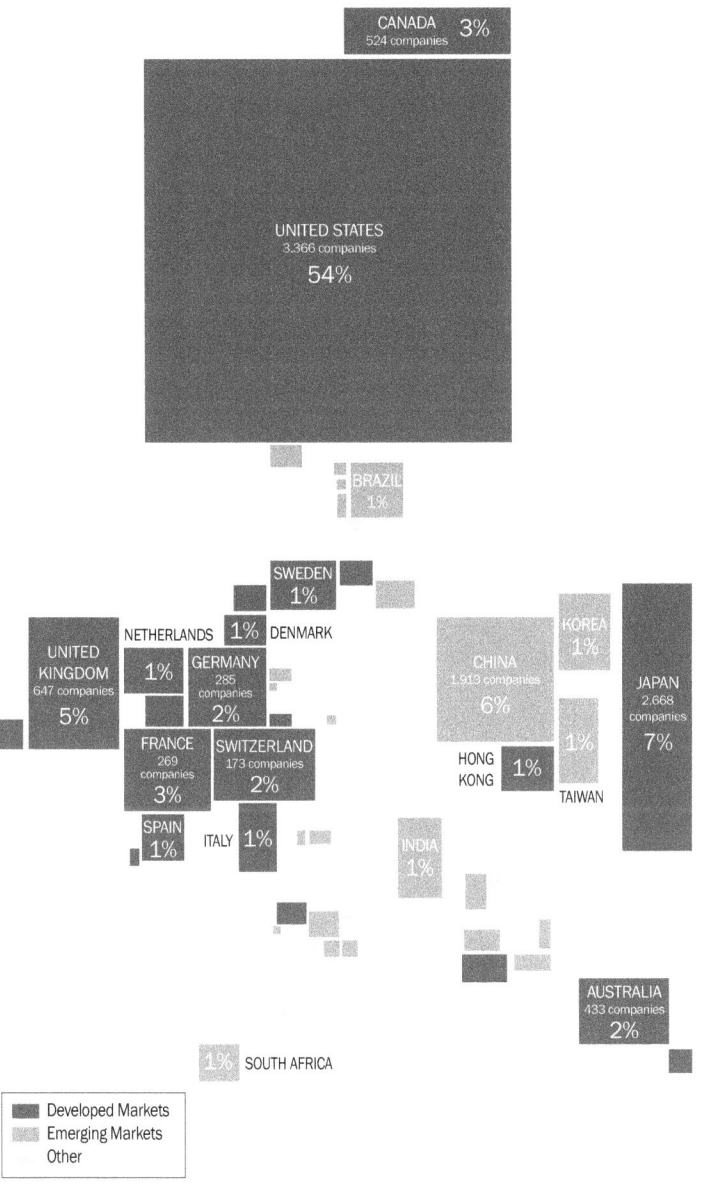

Figure 1 Per cent of world market capitalisation as at 31 December 2019.

smaller than Barclays. Research suggests that exposure to smaller companies improves diversification with higher expected returns over the longer term.

There is another dynamic in play, which involves someone's opinion. If a company's price is low compared to its book assets relative to similar companies, it could be considered a 'value company'. Conversely, a company with a high price ratio relative to peers could be considered a 'growth company'. Evidence suggests that investors that have greater exposure to value companies – ie companies that have cheaper stock prices relative to fundamentals such as book value – increase their expected returns over longer investment horizons.

Another way of valuing a company is through the price to earnings ratio 'P/E Ratio'. The P/E Ratio compares a company's share price and the actual company earnings on a per-share basis. We can look back at the trailing P/E Ratio which gives a historical insight into a company's valuation. We can also look at the forward P/E Ratio which takes a view and considers an opinion, on what may happen in the future. The P/E Ratio is a good way of determining if the current price of a company that doesn't own any physical assets is fair, for example a firm that just provides a service. Price to book (P/B) is more commonly used as a backwards-looking measure, as book values are relatively stable and simply look at just the assets less any liabilities within a company. We can see these dynamics below starting with Beta which is simply referring to the whole equity market by way of a starting point.

At the risk of stating the obvious, buying your own home and paying off your mortgage, if you have one, can also be considered an investment. Some people avoid thinking of their house as an investment to avoid focusing on it as part of an investment port-folio, as ultimately everyone needs a roof over their head. Commodities and precious metals can again be considered. The volatility of commodities can, however, outweigh their appropriateness as a safe portfolio asset, and they can also be difficult to access without the use of complicated derivatives, which I don't feel the need to explain, and would require a book of its own. Gold may or may not be a good safe-haven asset and, again, it suffers from high vola-tility with its value derived from its scarcity. Whilst it makes nice jewellery, it doesn't yield an income like bonds or equities. Other investments like digital currencies have become popular in recent times, and we will have to see if they one day feature alongside snake oil and tulips on Wikipedia searches.

Equities – the key drivers

- Company size (market capitalisation)

- Relative price (price/book value)

- Profitability (operating profits/book value)

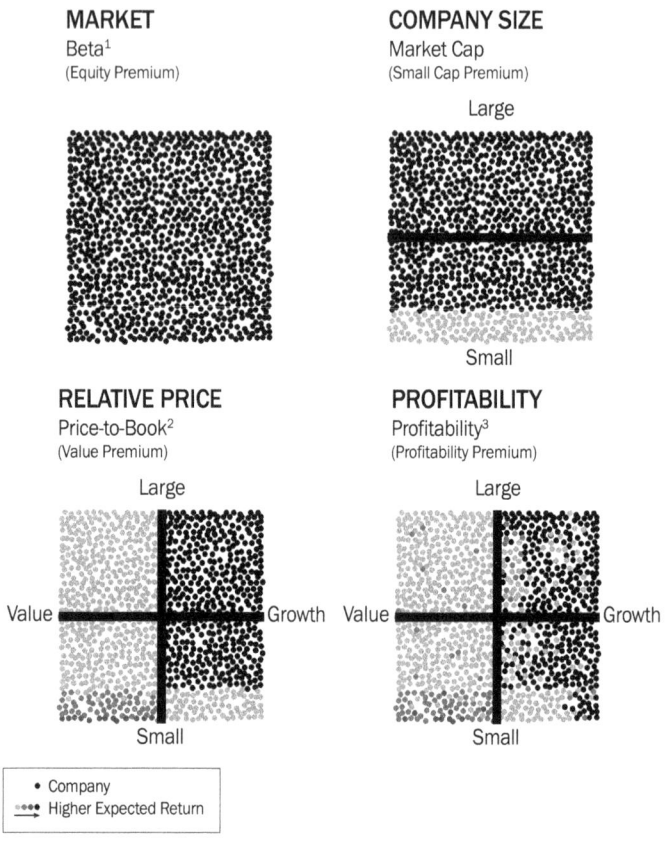

MARKET
Beta[1]
(Equity Premium)

COMPANY SIZE
Market Cap
(Small Cap Premium)

Large

Small

RELATIVE PRICE
Price-to-Book[2]
(Value Premium)

Large

Value — Growth

Small

PROFITABILITY
Profitability[3]
(Profitability Premium)

Large

Value — Growth

Small

• Company
•••• Higher Expected Return

Figure 2 Equity key drivers: Investors can pursue higher expected returns through a low-cost, well-diversified portfolio that targets these dimensions.

Notes: 1. Beta: A quantitative measure of the co-movement of a given stock, mutual fund, or portfolio with the overall market. 2. Price-to-book ratio: A company's capitalisation divided by its book value. It compares the market's valuation of a company to the value of that company as indicated on its financial statements. 3. Profitability: A measure of a company's current profits. We define this as operating income before depreciation and amortisation minus interest expense, scaled by book value.

As an aside, value presents an interesting conundrum. The suspension of the Woodford Equity Income Fund in 2019 demonstrates that failing to diversify properly can hurt: fund manager Neil Woodford came a cropper having bet the house on value for the last twenty-odd years, despite performing above his peers for many of those years. Markets work in the same way the world over, both in the developed and the emerging world. Typically, small-cap and value companies deliver higher returns than large-cap or growth companies.

Fixed income

Some securities you can invest in pay a fixed income. It's debt. Governments and companies borrow money, and you can lend it to them. Governments issue treasury bills (USA) and gilts (UK), and companies issue corporate bonds. You can buy them yourself, or buy a stake in a fund that holds them.

You might think your money is safe with governments, and technically it might be if you give it to the prime minister. But prime ministers are not particularly generous with what they give you back and it's likely that you'll get interest at around the same rate as inflation; so you can still buy your shopping next year. In other words, you'll stand still, more or less. Not particularly helpful in a rising-cost world.

Typically, companies will offer similar fixed rates if they are big and strong, so you'll have a similar end result. A new or smaller company may promise to pay you a higher rate, which sounds good. But because they have only just started, or don't have reserves as big as the government, or that large company, they might go bust and take your savings with them.

Within equity markets size, price and profitability are the dimensions of return. In fixed income markets the dimensions are term (when the company or government must repay your money), credit (of company or government) and currency in which the debt is denominated.

Table 3 *Dimensions of expected returns.*

Equities
Company Size (Market Capitalisation)
Relative Price[1] (Price/Book Equity)
Profitability[2] (Operating Profits/Book Equity)
Fixed income
Term (Sensitivity to Interest Rates)
Credit (Credit Quality of Issuer)
Currency (Currency of Issuance)

Notes: *1. Relative price is measured by the price-to-book ratio; value stocks are those with lower price-to-book ratios. 2. Profitability is measured as operating income before depreciation and amortisation minus interest expense, scaled by book value.*

We use a small selection of fixed income funds that we invest in for all clients, but we only use them to defend against equity movements. Think of them as a hedge – a safe haven to stop your £100,000 falling to £70,000 on paper when the equity market next falls. The more important dynamic to look at is the financial plan of the kind that we create for our clients, which accounts for the cyclical drops and recovery in equity values over time.

4

Styles of Investment

There are two different styles of investing at opposite ends of the spectrum: indexing (passive) and speculating (active).

Active investing – close your eyes and hope for the best?

In this case, a fund manager, your adviser or your broker acts on your behalf on a regular, perhaps daily, basis deciding on which stocks, shares and bonds you should buy, hold or sell. They attempt to forecast and pick what's hot and what's not, although (as I showed in Chapter Two) around eight out of ten times they will get it wrong. Effectively, these managers and the advisers behind them sit at the roulette table with your capital. The evidence suggests that the only winners will be the managers and advisers, who are gambling with your money.

Speculators rely on forecasting. Some would say diversification is simply for idiots who have no clue as to what stocks and bonds to pick, and often have a very low, or much lower level of diversification; all are confident they can pick the right investments, at the right time. They believe all they need to do is hold all the really great securities, stocks and bonds while avoiding the really bad ones. They pick funds with stars and crowns, quite often from a 'top twenty buy list', chase star managers and laugh at the index investor and passive managers who buy and hold whole markets for a gross 10% annualised return that might net down to 7% after inflation and fees.

The problem with the speculators' forecasting model is that, although many claim otherwise, no one can keep getting it right, let alone predict the next global depression, or five-year economic cycle when the markets might drop by 25%. They may win at times, but winners don't usually repeat. And what goes up 20% one year, may go down by 40% next year, at which point you will remind them that they told you they knew when to 'get you in' and 'back out again'.

If they lose 80% of the time, the figures they want you to focus on are the rewards when they do win,

20% of the time. It's human nature to be seduced by big numbers. When they do beat the index they track, investors tend to get overexcited and when the fund manager delivers a 47% return, investors pile more money in. Naturally, everybody then wants part of the action, which is great; but when you join at the top, after everybody else has already invested, the investment usually has only one way to go – down.

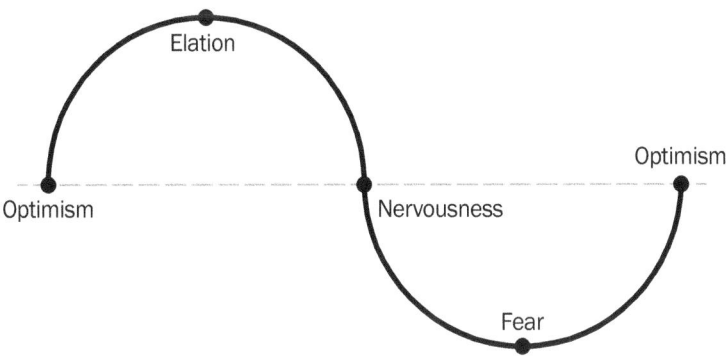

Figure 3 *Many investors follow their emotions*

Evidence shows that these massive successes do not repeat. In fact, they ultimately slide backwards. Therefore, be a little sceptical if you hear an adviser promising a huge return or spot a media announcement boasting of the same, because more often than not they are describing a one-off gain that generally will not be repeated year on year.

The financial press loves success stories about big returns and treats the glossy networks and their advisers as if they were caped superheroes. In my opinion, the financial press is complicit in the £64 billion a year problem as it relies on the noise generated by such success stories to sell copies and advertising space; it creates a co-dependent vicious circle.

The short-lived hype of every big fund story creates a buzz and elated investors jump in at the top, then panic, and in quick succession it all starts to go backwards: the inevitable sale follows, and fear sets in. People sell and crystallise losses. Then they move on to chase the next big fund or superhero manager. This is a reckless strategy that will cause long-term damage to your financial future. 'But hang on a minute,' I hear some people cry, 'there are rules and regulations in place. What about the Financial Conduct Authority with its checks and policing?'

Sadly, the FCA is also part of the problem. It is a very large institution with a main objective of ensuring 'markets function well'. Consumer protection is one of three sub-objectives, but this doesn't mean they are able to dedicate manpower to the issues I raise.[9] I expect that many of these issues are seen as insignificant, alongside other issues they battle with each day, such as fraud, scams and unauthorised advisers duping people into transferring guaranteed final salary pensions into Brazilian rainforest developments, and such like. It is also worth noting that the revenue onboarded by the FCA, from some of the large private banks and networks that I mention, is off the charts. To be clear, I would never suggest the FCA is in cahoots with these firms, or is turning a blind eye to the issues, rather that it just has far bigger fish to fry. If I come across as frustrated, I am. It's not just about the money, it's the principle of under-informing people who simply want to find peace of mind and security in their retirement.

This is about what's yours and what happens to it. Of course, you're free to make up your own mind, but who would want to gamble their future in the hope that 20% of the time you might win against a sure-fire 80% fail rate? Unless you simply dream that your hard-earned cash will somehow turn into pots of gold.

Passive investing – long-term buy and hold?

You can buy a stake in all the shares that make up a stock market index, such as the UK FTSE 100. These funds are commonly called tracker funds because by their very nature they track the market, effectively buying a stake in every listed company that is included in the index they choose to track. I shared in Chapter Two that the UK and US stock markets have both delivered returns of around 10% per annum since 1956. Just think about that for a moment.

You don't just have to track the FTSE 100. You may wish to track the UK small-cap market. That's grown by around 15% per annum since 1956.[10] The value-cap market hasn't shone any great light in the decade since 2010 but again, going back to 1956, its annual delivery has been around 12%. You can invest passively in the UK and also in global markets, including the emerging markets. With passive investing there's no interest in any particular company, or any one sector, such as healthcare, banking or agriculture. The individual sectors are of no significance, it's a major slice of the market, top to toe, that's being tracked and that's what counts.

While active managers rummage around the available data and work themselves into a lather, trying to identify agricultural companies to hold, or sell, the passive manager sits back, trusts in nearly seven decades of evidence and buys all of the shares that make up the index, in the knowledge that some will fail, and some will thrive. The passive manager doesn't try to manage a selection of stocks, or focus on the brands they personally like or have confidence in.

Because of this approach the passive manager aims to achieve the market return, whatever that is, whereas the active manager will often fail to keep pace with the same index because they choose badly four times out of five. Added to that, the active manager and their funds usually charge more, so the compound effect is two-fold. The active manager loses the battle, and the charges drag the fund down further.

As a passive investor you should retain the investment through all market fluctuations and refrain from dabbling and guesswork. Speculating is the exact opposite, using forecasting to try to repeat short-term gains by moving your money around.

It is important that you understand the fundamental difference between the two approaches and grasp what diversification of investments really means, and what it should look like. The long-term outcomes of these approaches can seriously affect your long-term finances, and as a result, your financial liquidity throughout retirement.

We saw in Chapter Two that in the UK around £7.7 trillion is held in pensions, ISAs and general investments. When one of the big (and expensive) investment advice firms or network operators wants to sign you up, they may claim that they can deliver performance and premiums using a selection of actively managed funds. Remember, 80% of actively managed funds shrink. It beggars belief that some advisers effectively look in a rear-view mirror and then guess what might happen in the future. But a fund that has just had a great year probably will not repeat that performance in two years' time. The evidence strongly suggests that 'luck' does not repeat.[11]

Ignoring the noise and focusing on running with a passive fund might seem boring, but this approach delivers, time and time again. History has also shown us that we can achieve more than the market return in the long term if we try to track not only large-cap companies but also growth-cap, small-cap and value-cap shares. I call this full factor diversification. It extends a portfolio's exposure to more than one type of equity share, and if we can do this in both the developed world and the emerging world we buy in further layers of asset, sector and geographic diversification.

I explain to clients that doing this will expose their capital to all markets, buy every type of listed stock on the planet and hold them all indefinitely with a passive investing, or indexing strategy. We buy stakes in large-cap, small-cap, growth-cap and value-cap funds, throughout the developed world. We repeat this in the emerging world and when doing so we do not worry whether China will beat India, or Latin America will outperform the Pacific Basin.

In more recent times we have departed from the 'strictly passive' approach by adding socially responsible investment funds so that we capture envisaged returns from companies that will make a difference to our children's lives. Funds with environmental, social and governance (ESG) filters measure the sustainability and societal impact of the companies they invest in and help determine the financial performance of a business.

However, ESG is not a perfect 'science'. For example, oil producer Exxon Mobil is one of the world's biggest investors in renewable energy. If you're an investor who's passionate about protecting the planet from climate change, do you withhold your capital out of principle, or trust in capitalism to act for the greater good by continuing to supply capital to such a company?

In general, we think that if companies have a sustainable outlook, it gives them a greater chance of success than if they don't. By investing in funds that take a view on these matters, we see those funds as a further risk management strategy within the portfolio. We believe ESG funds are a step in the right direction. They have performed well, are diversified and have filters that exclude the world's worst behaved companies.

Operating in this way and maintaining low fees, it's far more likely (and we have proved this) to achieve good, consistent results, year on year. The passive adviser, whose *modus operandi* is to sustain a client throughout their whole retirement, checks the data book and sees the opportunities straight ahead.

Table 4 Annualised rates of returns (%)[12]

Annualised rates of return (%)	5 years	10 years	20 years	50 years
	2015–2019	*2010–2019*	*2000–2019*	*1970–2019*
Inflation: UK Retail Price Index	2.5	3.0	2.8	5.8
UK One-Month Treasury Bills	0.4	0.4	2.4	6.8
DFA* UK Market Index	7.5	8.1	5.0	11.5
DFA* UK Value Cap Index	6.6	6.9	4.7	13.4
DFA* UK Small Cap Index	10.0	12.9	9.7	15.2
DFA* Global Core Equity Index	12.4	12.4	8.4	_
DFA* Global Targeted Value Index	10.5	11.7	11.7	_
DFA* Global Small Cap Index	11.5	12.6	10.7	14.7
DFA* Emerging Core Equity Index	9.3	6.9	9.9	_
DFA* Emerging Targeted Value Index	9.3	6.6	11.9	_
DFA* Emerging Small Cap Index	9.8	7.5	10.4	_
DFA* US Large Cap Index (in USD)	8.6	12.4	8.2	13.1
DFA* US Small Cap Index (in USD)	7.8	12.4	10.1	12.4

*Dimensional

CASE STUDY: DEREK AND ANNABEL

Derek and Annabel, approaching retirement, were concerned that the funds they had been advised some years earlier to leave in a fixed income investment plan (70% of their money) had not increased in value. With over £730,000 in pensions they were uncertain whether they had enough to see them comfortably through their old age. They had put their trust in a household name you'd regularly see advertise in the financial pages of the Sunday papers. This big brand had placed £425,000 of Derek and Annabel's money in a fixed income fund because the adviser told them it was a safe bet. In some respects, that's true, but by its very nature ('fixed') it was simply going to stagnate.

Each year the 70% of Derek and Annabel's money in the fixed income fund was increasing (a bit), while the 30% they held in equities decreased. This strategy, which we will discuss in more detail in Chapter Seven, is called 'lifestyling' and is designed to move increasing proportions of a pension fund from 'risky' equity investments into 'safe' fixed income investments as retirement approaches and then beyond retirement. I'd contend that this was far from a safe bet because inflation was chipping away at that pot of money daily.

If we look back to the 1950s, inflation was running at 5% per annum. It may well be around 2.5% in 2020 but you have to look at what it might be over the next thirty years. The 70% invested in fixed income stocks would have plummeted, in real value. Not only were Derek and Annabel losing money in real terms, there was also no possibility of them ever living the retirement life they hoped for.

Worse, we realised that the remaining 30% in equities was languishing idly in a prehistoric 'with profits' fund. These funds were popular in the 1970s when they offered protection against poor equity performance and inflation was running high. They were designed to smooth out the highs and lows of the markets, keeping money back in good years to maintain returns in a leaner period. However, today markets aren't growing at the same exponential rates as in the heady days of the 1980s.

Therefore, while 'with profits' funds were designed with the best intentions, the guarantees they provided have recently been poor value for the (mostly hidden) charges paid. Derek and Annabel instinctively knew there had to be a better way for their money to work for them, and they were right.

The first thing I suggested was reversing their bond and equity ratio with 70% held in equity. At first, they were concerned that this meant embracing more risk, and it was my job to help them accept that movement (both up and down) is a normal part of their money's growth path, counterintuitive as that seemed at the time.

They soon realised that what I've since exposed them to is not risk, it's simply a series of price movements, during which any falls have always been temporary, whereas the rises have always resumed eventually; and that a fund that has grown more in the good years can sustain falls better than one that has stagnated. It became abundantly clear to them that if they continued to tie up a major part of their investments in bonds generating low income, they'd be more likely to outlive their money (the big question for everyone being 'Will I outlive my money, or will my money outlive me?').

The biggest gain, however, can't always be measured in financial terms. For Derek and Annabel, it was the confidence that they could live life on their terms, without compromises, whatever happens with the markets, in the knowledge that when markets do fall, which they will, this doesn't mean they will lose money so long as they sit tight (a major difference between passive and active strategies), remain calm and wait for markets to rebound. Derek and Annabel know how much they need and that it should be there when they need it because inside their financial plan we have factored in the crashes that seem to come along every seven years or so, and temporarily melt around 25% of our capital when they do. While these depreciations are unfortunate and none of us like to see them, we also know that the markets always rebound eventually, and that these temporary revaluations are not the end of the world.

To find certainty we need clarity, which I will discuss in greater depth in Part Four. When, after working with me for some time, the penny drops and clients are reassured about their future security, it's an emotional moment for me as well as for them: I can see on the clients' faces that they realise 'We're going to be okay'.

Given that certainty and peace of mind are uppermost in our subconscious desires for a long-lasting, sustainable retirement, we need to redefine what we consider to be a win when we make financial decisions. I suggest that being able to rest safely in the knowledge that the money won't run out is a win. To achieve that, our money needs to be exposed, in the main, passively – to capture the way the whole market moves. Placing our trust in a series of knee-jerk guesses or in how two different companies in the same sector will perform is a fruitless exercise.

Nick Murray, a veteran investment professional in the USA, can often be heard arguing that money market purists direct 95% of their effort and energy towards trying to predict what will happen in 5% of the market. He actually says 'they spend a hugely disproportionate amount of their time trying to be right, rather than in doing good'.[13]

I couldn't agree more. They're focused on those almost irrelevant, tiny little movements that alone won't make the difference, whereas that difference is achieved when you go all in and track the large-cap and small-cap, and the growth-cap and value-cap equity markets, in both the developed and developing world, with low costs. Then stay the course and don't panic just because markets tank every seven years or so. Leave everything you've bought where it is, and it will bounce back. And if you can pump more in when prices are low, do it.

Market growth performance trends 1956–2020

In Figure 4 we can see the growth of £1 from 1956 to 2019 if invested in the UK main equity market, and the small-cap and value-cap markets, measured against inflation and UK gilts (bonds/fixed income).

It's the evidence I show clients in order to instil confidence and trust when investing their capital – be this within a pension, ISA, investment bond or other such 'wrapper'. Remember they are just 'products'. What goes inside the wrapper, in my opinion, is the important information.

The results speak for themselves and show the returns that can be earned just by tracking those markets. Any investment manager that's busy showing you how hard they're working for you and your money and claiming they can 'get in when it's low' and 'jump back out' as soon as shares head in the other direction

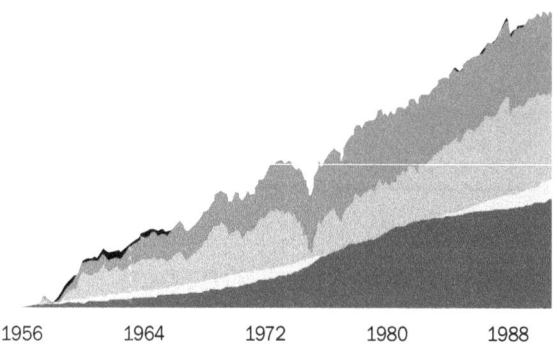

Figure 4 Let markets work for you: growth of a pound, 1956–2019 (compounded monthly).

is probably not being entirely truthful and doing you a profound disservice.

They are the market junkies who thrive on guesswork and adrenalin, best avoided in my mind. I very much doubt they share the values of their hard-working clients or have any of their clients' real hopes and dreams for their retirement in mind.

If the market junkies were interested in really helping their clients, one might think they would adopt the passive strategy and trust in the data. But why would they? Their model relies on the opposite strategy: market timing and guesswork. And in any event, their own futures will be just fine because each year they're extracting an extra 1.4%, £64 billion, from their

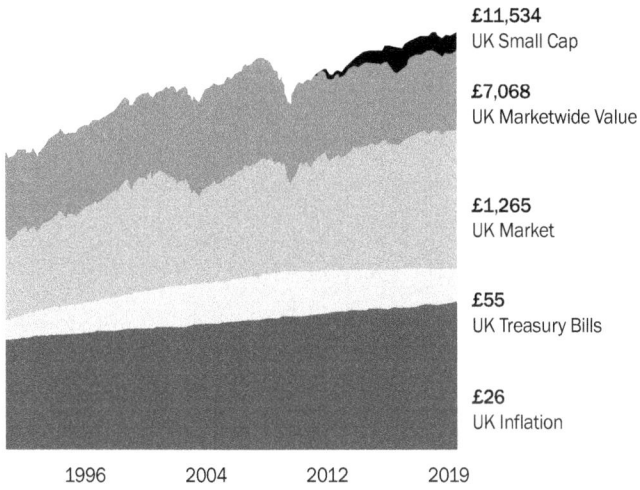

£11,534
UK Small Cap

£7,068
UK Marketwide Value

£1,265
UK Market

£55
UK Treasury Bills

£26
UK Inflation

1996   2004   2012   2019

clients into their profit and loss account and nothing that happens inside your portfolio changes that.

So a lot of the advice you are getting may not be that good. Sorry to be the bearer of bad news, but that's how it is. In Part Three we will look further at the problems bad advice causes when you are planning for the future.

PART THREE

WHAT'S YOUR PLAN?

5

Have You Made a Plan?

What moves me most is when clients share their worries and concerns about how to plan properly for their future. Or, as is more often the case, when they're scared by their inability to plan at all. Worse still is when they gradually realise that the plan they had thought was the right course of action is not worth the paper it's written on. Such clients often see me as an emergency service, hoping that I can resuscitate their dream future. Sometimes I can, but sometimes I can't.

I occasionally meet people who have everything locked down. Probably one in ten do. But most of the time one of three plans is always present:

- No plan

- Bad plan

- Wrong plan

Of the remaining nine out of ten I would say most have no plan. It's likely that if you are reading this book, one of these predicaments will apply to you.

Part Three will outline the characteristics of each of these 'plans' and introduce you to my model, CLEARER™, which in Part Four will guide you through the process of formulating a new, workable plan that you can rely on.

If you follow my model, you'll be able to create a tailored plan and investment portfolio that works for you. If nothing else, the CLEARER™ model will prompt you to think about the various important considerations necessary to achieve your goals. Only then will you be in a position to plan your retirement with clarity.

That all requires you to start thinking with the end in mind. It's crucial that you have sufficient funds to cover your essential costs before you even consider the 'fun money' for treats and holidays. And there's no point investing in a bad plan or the wrong plan.

It's not simply a matter of coasting and hoping for the best. You'd be surprised how many people don't really understand how much money they're going to need when they retire. Life costs far more than we think it does and people rarely take inflation into account.

Chances are that, by thirty years after you have retired, your income will need to be 2.5 times higher than it was at the start of your retirement. Inflation has averaged around 5% per annum since 1956. The Retail Price Index (RPI) shows it's been around 2.6% for the past ten years, though many of us may feel this understates real changes in the cost of living.

I have four children aged 23, 15, 12 and 10, and it feels like we experience 8% inflation whenever we try to take the children out for dinner or on holiday. Often, I hear of people's reserves running low in retirement because they haven't planned well, and their having to 'turn the taps down'. I can't think of anything worse for them after their forty-plus years spent working. Poor souls. These people had no plan. They were lost at sea, trying to navigate life with a broken compass. They didn't know how much money was going to be enough to get them through retirement. And they ran out. They know how much they need now, of course, being dependent on the state. They might have a basic state pension coming in at around £9,000 per annum but the children have to pay for them when they go out for dinner. Sad.

Many people who have already retired are taking what they need from their pot, not really understanding how long it will last. Some will crack on, close one eye and just keep every finger and toe crossed. They will either run out or perhaps just about scrape over the line. Who knows? They don't because they haven't got a plan. Others think what they have is enough yet may never feel reassured that they have done their sums properly. They don't know either. Some are no doubt afraid to check it out and get advice.

At the other end of the spectrum, people sometimes live frugally and prevent themselves from living a comfortable life despite the fact they *do* have enough money; they just don't realise this. That's also because they have no plan.

Therefore, the aim of this chapter is to encourage you to reset your financial compass so that you can navigate towards a more certain financial future. We'll look at each problematic planning scenario in turn.

Most of the people I meet might have an idea around what retirement may look like but in the vast majority of cases they haven't actually written down any figures or worked out exactly what it's going to cost. And that's assuming today's 2.6% continues; but what if, in twenty years' time, inflation rises to double digits? How are these people going to manage the extended retirement we can now look forward to, possibly up to the age of 100 and beyond? What if they don't have a clue how much money they'll need each year, not just to live, but to do all those things they'd like to do?

In addition, there are other issues to consider around general financial and estate planning: for example the UK's mass apathy about succession planning, a lack of protection against potential catastrophes such as premature death or serious illness, and our failure to use our annual tax breaks and allowances.

There are many reasons why people have no idea and no plan. Many recognise that they need a plan but don't know where to start. They can be paralysed with fear at the rising cost of living, so simply keep their fingers crossed and hope for the best. Others feel ground down by financial institutions' and advisers' relentless attempts to sell them stuff they don't need. Some no longer feel cared for and don't know where to turn or who to trust. The result is apathy, and they do nothing. Who can blame them?

Then there are those whose future is one thing too many to worry about in their busy lives, something they will deal with tomorrow. They labour under the misconception that there's nothing they can do about their retirement anyway. They also have no plan. Or maybe their business is their pension – most of the time a classic *faux pas*.

Some rely on their existing pension provider or employer without investigating whether their savings will provide them enough money. Turning back to existing providers, a good many of you out there may think you must settle for the first offer on the table from a big-name provider. You don't have to. Any decent independent financial adviser who puts their clients' needs first is able to work on other 'open market' options, taking a wider view of the overall position. Maybe existing arrangements can be transferred into a new plan, where the investments work better and projections are provided that can be tracked continually throughout a three-decade retirement.

Others think the state will cover them. But the state welfare provision was set up in the 1940s to manage 34 million people who mostly died by the age of 68. Today there are 67 million of us, all living well into our 80s and 90s. How can the state make provision in 15 or 20 years' time for today's 50-year-olds? After paying for all of the government's COVID-19 bailouts of 2020?

Death isn't the only certainty in life, so is the rising cost of living. What might cost £5 today could cost £12.50 in the thirtieth year of your retirement. That money your existing pension provider has told you will be your total future income may end up looking pretty poor once the compound effects of inflation have been factored in.

That's where the plan falls apart, and you have no plan. Your pension provider may have projected your future pension income, but will it really see you through? You may have been told your pension fund will offer you an annuity, but rates are low at the moment. This might leave you wondering what the point in that was.

| 1972 | 2020 |
| 3p | 76p |

Back in 1972 – the year of the silver wedding (and when I was born), a first-class stamp was just 3p. Today in 2020 the same first-class stamp (it no longer has the price on it) is 76p. Thirty years ago in 1990 (a typical retirement window) the price of a first-class stamp was 22p. Today, it is over three times more expensive than it was back then, and it's likely that the same three-fold rise will happen over the next thirty years, because that's what inflation does to us.[14] This is really important because, for example, if you spend £5,000 on a holiday now, it will likely cost you £15,000 in thirty years' time, at the same time it will cost £2.28 to put a letter in the post. Let's think about this and consider what you might see over your three-decade retirement if you were to look back.

Table 5 *The increase in price of a first-class stamp*

3p	12p	17p	22p	25p	27p	30p	41p	63p	76p
1972	1980	1985	**1990**	**1995**	**2000**	**2005**	**2010**	**2015**	**2020**

The plan may have been stifled because it was heavily exposed to fixed income securities (see Chapter Seven). The irony is that the risk-averse baby boom generation has fallen into a false sense of security about investment asset classes. In fact, the greater risk could lie in losing actual purchasing power as a result of being in fixed income investments.

The good news is that an independent financial adviser can help steer people away from *plat du jour* standard pension arrangements and devise a plan to fix this, as long as they can get to the root of the problem early enough. As I showed in Chapter Three, by exposing your funds to all classes of global equities (as opposed to fixed income) there's a greater chance you will be able to keep pace with the rising cost of living over three decades. In my experience, strategy makes all the difference to plans and can accelerate growth exponentially.

Robust client-focused advisers will always deploy their toolbox and study the individual's current expenditure to break down every aspect of lifestyle costs, from essentials through to luxuries. The adviser then looks ahead to see what expenses can be expected to change at retirement – such as no longer needing to make mortgage repayments or support children's living and education expenses.

The adviser looks at what the client currently spends and projects it forward; determines whether they will still need the same; and then calculates the magic number: the amount needed to maintain you through retirement, living life to the full without running out of money. Or dying with too much. More on that later, in Chapter Twelve.

Whilst baby boomers are perhaps lucky, some would say, in that they were able to buy property before prices rose through the roof while incomes stayed flat-tish, their money can be squeezed in other ways. They probably have children in their 20s and 30s who find it difficult to buy their own properties; they may also be caring for and supporting parents in their 80s.

I was born in 1972, six years after the baby boom generation. Most of us who fit into the Generation X box are unlikely to benefit from the final salary pension schemes our parents belonged to, and as parents we too expect to have to help adult children with house deposits, education costs and general support. Thanks to increasing life expectancy, our responsibility for our parents will typically continue longer, so it's little wonder that it's difficult and stressful to think about making provision for our own retirement. We have one eye on our children and the other on our parents.

CASE STUDY: PETER

Peter was 44 when he came to Wilcocks. He wanted to retire at 60. Achieving the level of income in retirement that he desired looked a long shot at first, and we calculated that he was set to run out of money within five years of retirement. The lighter grey bars you see in Figure 6, that kick in as the balance drops below zero, represent him essentially going into an imaginary overdraft each year. In the sixth year of his retirement, he would run dry. In Figures 6 and 7, the total numbers showing the positive and negative balances on the left are exaggerated by the effect of inflation.

In reality, the £60,000 annual income he needed to take him from age 60 to a planned ripe old age of 90, at a flat rate would have added up to £1.8 million. But with inflation of 2.9% a year (RPI) factored in, the £60,000 needed to rise to more than £130,000 in his ninetieth year. We can see this in action if we look at how inflation over the last 30 years would have affected £60,000.

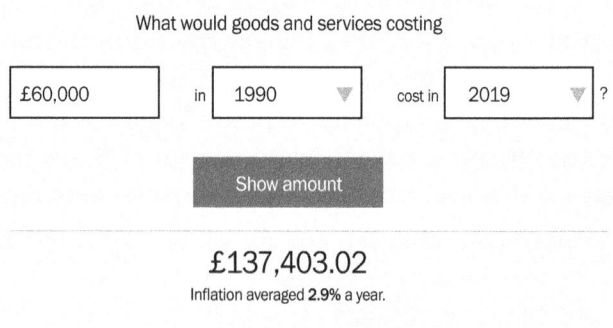

Figure 5 *Effect of inflation*[15]

Peter's income needs might decrease at age 75 and he might not need anything like that, but I'm using this example because it exaggerates the point and makes us think. In this case, we established that the income taken from his business needed to be higher for the period from age 44 until retirement at 60 so we factored that in and adapted the plan accordingly.

It still wasn't enough and with £60,000 per year coming out our projection still showed he would need the imaginary overdraft five years later, from age 70. We ended up with a plan for a staggered retirement that began by slowing down at age 60. I don't have a magic wand, but I can help people see the real picture. Rather than being a ship at sea with no compass, at the very least they can navigate through choppy waters and still reach their destination. Figure 7 shows how the plan looked once we had finished, and still looked the last time I saw Peter.

He can get to age 85 now before he has to worry about running out or having to adjust his lifestyle. In reality he probably won't need as much from 75, as I said above. That's great, because it allows us to plan ahead, and stress-test the model. You can see that this projection even extends his life to age 100. Who knows – he's certainly got one thing less to worry about.

It's also worth mentioning that we took Peter out of a plan that was both bad and wrong. He was paying excessive fees on a network pension, ISA and general investment account that, in my opinion, was overexposed in fixed income. Utter madness at age

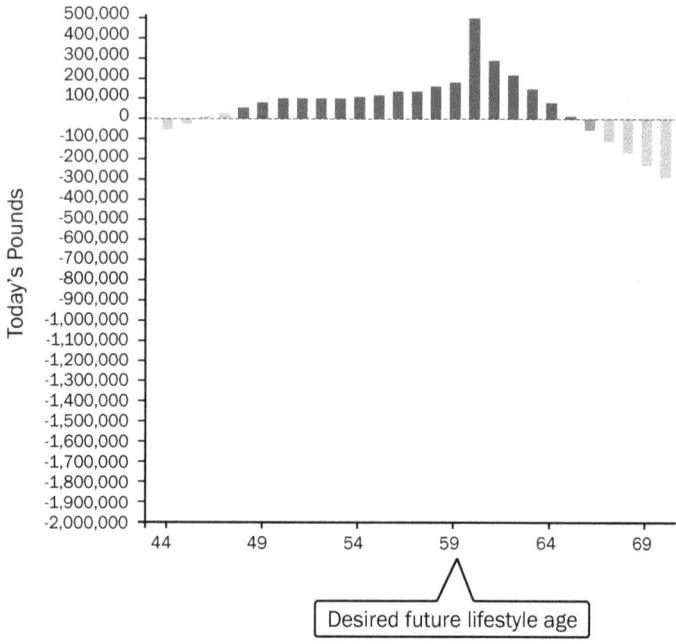

Figure 6 Peter's starting plan

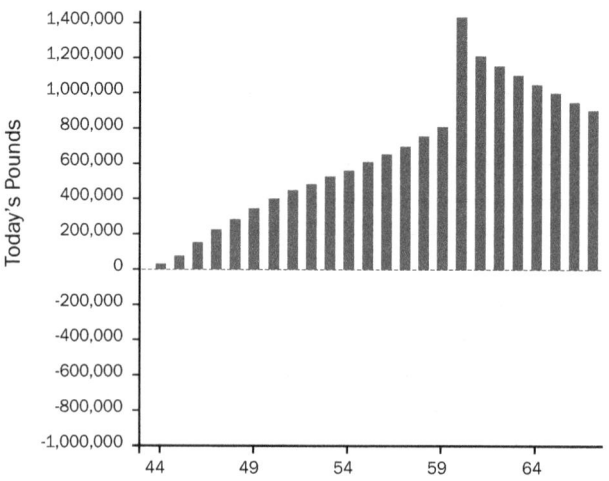

Figure 7 Peter's final plan

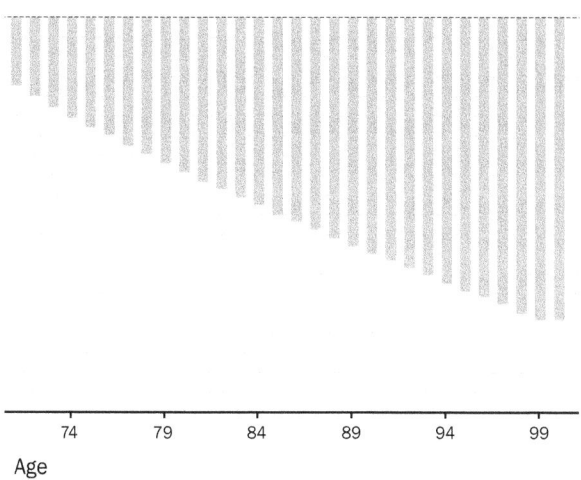

Age

74 79 84 89 94 99

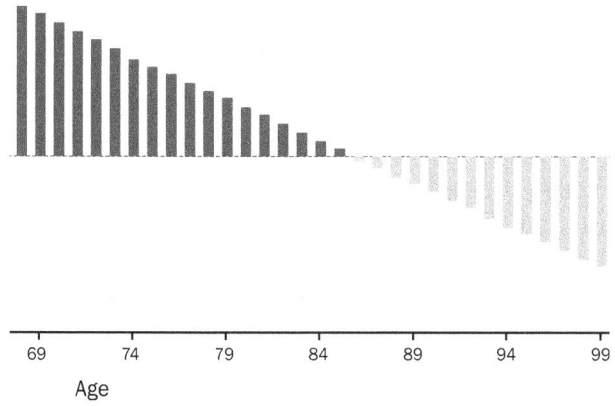

Age

69 74 79 84 89 94 99

44. We handled the transfer of his existing assets to a new arrangement, as well as helping him prepare the financial plan.

I'm not in any position to offer any financial advice until I've put in time working out who I'm talking to and what they want. By the time I come to giving regulated financial and investment advice I've built up a solid picture of my client based on grass-roots knowledge. They, in turn, have also invested trust in me. Only now can I consider what financial products and investments might be best suited to deliver the client's financial plan, one that I hope we will co-manage for the whole of their lifetime, through the good times and the not-so-good. Ideally, the financial plan would show the bars increasing in size over time, indicating a growing positive balance, to support a lifestyle without compromise and hopefully an ultimate legacy to loved ones or other beneficiaries.

No plan? Don't panic!

You might be feeling nervous if you've realised you don't have a plan in place. At the end of this section, I'll walk you through the key points of my CLEARER™ model, which will turn things around and give you the confidence to push ahead. The good independent financial planner has your interests at heart.

Start now: go to my website and download the life planning questionnaire (www.martinwilcocks.co.uk/flp). It will get you considering:

- What would be a good income to retire on?

- Who will be spending it with you and should you plan jointly?

- When should retirement start and what should it look like throughout?

- Why is this important? How would you feel if you missed the boat?

- How much will it cost initially and by how much will this have to increase each year?

My questionnaire includes three challenging questions that might seem like short, sharp shocks to some: I ask clients to imagine and describe their ideal retirement. Then some bad news arrives. It's designed to make us think about what to do with our remaining time and what our future self will most regret not doing or experiencing. In this way I steer clients towards thinking about personal fulfilment, and other things that might have been deeply buried inside them for years.

It also replaces the fear of not making, or having a plan, with certainty and knowing exactly what it is you have to work with. It needn't paint a grim picture, because with the right help and advice, there's always scope for improvement.

Do this planning now while you are strong, healthy and resilient because you are your most important asset, and nobody can take that away from you. Unfortunately, unforeseen accidents, events and ill health can.

Of our current clients:

- Most had no 'number' worked out (the annual income they wanted to retire on) when they first came to us.

- Some are now doing something different vocationally than when they first came to us.

- With every new client, we have been able to find at least one area to tighten up or to make good from scratch.

Some more numbers:

- Around 30 million adults in the UK haven't made a will and will die intestate.

- Some 23,000 people a year apply to the Court of Protection because their loved ones need someone to act on their behalf but no power of attorney is in place.

- About £5.2 billion was collected in inheritance tax in 2020, paid by people who failed to plan properly for it.

- It has been estimated that the amount of cover families should have to protect them against disaster and catastrophe scenarios is some £1.5 trillion short of what it ought to be.

- Each year, £360 billion in standard basic tax allowances that could be claimed, through for example simple but effective ISA and pension plans, is not claimed.

6

Have You Made a Bad Plan?

A bad plan is, literally, the £64 billion problem. In Chapter Two I explained how investing with any of the glossy networks or private banks can come with a high price tag and that around 80% of the time they fail to deliver meaningful long-term returns. In fact, their high charges drag the funds downwards.

Bad plans can be the result of misplaced trust in big institutions that sell you a dream of your future. Many decent people work within those institutions, but a large, rotten core exists at the heart of the apple.

If you've been sold a plan by an active fund manager or an adviser who promotes active funds, then four times out of five it's a bad plan; as I showed in Chapter Two, 80% of these funds perform poorly and fail to outperform a relative benchmark such as the FTSE 100 Index. Yet sales pitches to clients are based on past performance that may never repeat. It has already happened. I suggest that a 7% annual return, after deducting fees and inflation, while it might not sound so exciting, is far more dependable over twenty-five to thirty years.

The problem is, every year there's always a new kid on the block, a shiny new fund. And eight out of ten times, it fails to outperform a simple benchmark. Eventually. The bad plan ignores the evidence. If you like to gamble serious amounts of money, then I'll take a guess that the rest of this chapter (and book) isn't for you.

Of course, evidence will show that active management can, and does, work effectively around 20% of the time, but remember that even if your active funds are and have been performing exceptionally well for one, two or even three years, bad years *always* come. It is inevitable that at some point your actively managed fund will underperform.

If your investments, pensions or ISAs are managed by one of the glossy networks or someone else pushing active funds you pay around 3%, on average, in charges and fees. This eats into your pot of money. And whether you win or lose, your advisers are guaranteed their share of that £64 billion every year.

While their occasional wins may be big, so can their losses; in the very rare event that a loss wiped out your portfolio completely, you would still have to pay the manager's fees. I don't believe it's a safe way to manage money that's supposed to support you through three or more decades of retirement.

The slow and steady approach proves its reliability time and again. Here is my seven-point cross-check to use when active fund advisers or managers turn on the charm in the hope of persuading you to sign on their dotted line:

The seven-point cross-check

1. What do they do differently to deliver consistent, positive results?

2. How long has the fund been operational and what's the track record?

3. What are the trading charges?

4. What are the active manager's charges?

5. What's the total expense ratio for this particular fund?

6. What do they charge for the supporting financial advice every year?

7. What makes their fund different to the 80% of active funds that fail, and have repeatedly been proved to fail?

Depending on their responses, and subject to verification, the plan might just begin to look like a bad one compared to a steadier, evidence-tested approach. Some financial advisers or wealth managers may also deploy a 'discretionary fund/investment manager' (DFM) to assist them. This will add another layer of cost, and another relationship to juggle. It can all be spun to sound good. Take care. Your investment should not be made to sound so complicated that it can only be handled by an 'expert'.

An untested actively managed fund may not have a track record and it has been proven that active fund managers cannot consistently predict outcomes, good or bad. The evidence suggests that their process is based largely on guesswork. Does this sound like a good plan to you? You might as well walk into any betting shop and hand over all of your cash, savings and pension funds to the cashier.

Stock picker Neil Woodford earned his early reputation at Invesco Perpetual. Those who bought into his success by investing £10,000 into a Woodford pension fund in the late 1980s would have seen that increase to £250,000 in just over twenty-five years. Who wouldn't be swayed by those kinds of results? A 7% return would have taken the same £10,000 to around £60,000 over the same period.

In his most recent venture one of his funds dropped sharply and a large number of investors pulled out, with a few stragglers left holding rapidly depreciating units when the fund was suspended by its administrator. I'm not singling out Woodford, but his actively managed approach exemplifies, albeit in the extreme, the inherent risks that I associate with a bad plan. The wins may be visible, but always be prepared for disaster lurking around the corner. How can a temporary feeling of elation compare with the long-term damage caused by a catastrophic crash?

Is that gamble worth sacrificing your 70th birthday celebration or diamond wedding gathering for? How does it feel to be unable to fund your children through university, or pay for the care you need in your twilight years? Around 2,000 baby boomers currently retire every day, and they need to pay attention, if not for their own sake, then for the legacies they wish to leave behind.

I hold active fund managers largely responsible for the £7.6 trillion gap that existed in our UK retirement plans according to the Office for National Statistics in 2018. They estimated the gross pension liabilities accrued to date by UK pension providers in respect of employment-related (workplace) pensions and state pensions totalled £7.6 trillion. Ironically, this is the same figure as the amount we have invested.

Actively managed investments rely on win, win, win, but are usually followed by lose, lose, lose. It's an unpredictable rollercoaster ride. Yet some investors are willing to hire active managers because they realise that a 6% or 7% per year return will never cover the gap in their retirement plans, and they hope to achieve 12% or 14% per year: for the next twenty years! Before too long a bad plan is hatched and the adviser proceeds

to charge them 1% for the funds, 1% for the management and 1% for the products. Some advisers work for
networks that have higher initial fees – anything up to
6% – and lock-in clauses at the same 6%.

Now the clients are in worse shape than ever. In reality
they'd be better advised to save on holidays and eating
out in order to put aside an extra amount each month
into a pension or ISA. That is far more bearable than the
pain an active fund manager is prepared to inflict, in
the knowledge that every seven years or so the markets
will drop temporarily by 25% or 30%. An active fund
manager may suggest their model protects their investors from the cyclical 25–30% 'loss', a key word which
I will return to. Active fund managers and advisers
do not build their models based on the principle of
remaining calm during a fall. They might explain that
their strategy helps navigate the volatility by switching
clients' money in and out of the right assets, at the right
time, even though (as I showed in Chapter Two) this is
only successful approximately 20% of the time.

The more measured approach I advocate advises clients
that while it's impossible to predict with any certainty
future rise and falls of the markets, most of the time
those fluctuations are unimportant. Over sixty-five
years, the FTSE 100 Index, for example, might drop
25% every seven or so years, but it always recovers
eventually (see Figure 4). The gains have always been
recovered, so you might regard them as permanent,
while the declines have always been temporary, even
though twice in the last century that period has been

a long one. And on that journey, it is crucial to always remember one other piece of detail. What I am about to say next should be written on your bedstead. Never be out of the market. Missing just one or more of the best days throughout the last thirty years was catastrophic.

The following graph shows the performance of the S&P 500 Index, 1990–2019.

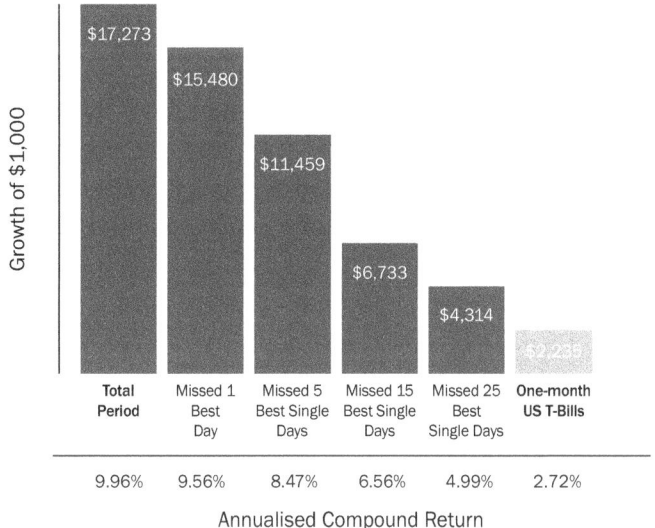

Figure 8 Reacting can hurt performance: missing only a few days of strong returns can drastically impact overall performance.

Notes: *Past performance is not a guarantee of future results. In US dollars. For illustrative purposes. The missed best day(s) examples assume that the hypothetical portfolio fully divested its holdings at the end of the day before the missed best day(s), held cash for the missed best day(s), and reinvested the entire portfolio in the S&P 500 at the end of the missed best day(s). Annualised returns for the missed best day(s) were calculated by substituting actual returns for the missed best day(s) with zero. S&P data © 2020 S&P Dow Jones Indices LLC, a division of S&P Global. All rights reserved. "One-Month US T- Bills" is the IA SBBI US 30 Day TBill TR USD, provided by Ibbotson Associates via Morningstar Direct. Data is calculated off rounded daily index values. Indices are not available for direct investment. Their performance does not reflect the expenses associated with the management of an actual portfolio.*

Investors who understand such evidence then stay the course when the market drops by 25% and other people panic and cash out. My advice in this situation is simple. Raid your reserves and invest more whilst the market is low because eventually the market will bounce back. I can't control the FTSE or Dow indices, or the emerging world stock markets, but I know that for the past sixty-five years they have delivered approximately 10% per annum, through good times, bad times and through the very worst of times.

Even the financial crisis that began in 2008 didn't make any difference to the long-term average, and whilst the markets might fall, the stocks within them usually continue to deliver dividends. In fairness, we have yet to see a full market recovery from the COVID-19 pandemic, but based on the past sixty-five years, I trust that it will bounce back, maybe even by the time this book is published, and then continue on its permanent advance. Let me offer something that most financial advisers might be reluctant to put their name to: I guarantee that it will, I just can't guarantee when.

My clients understand that a 'loss' only occurs when you sell; a fall in the index, no matter how spectacular, is simply a temporary decline. They rest easy in the knowledge that the value of their portfolio will eventually come back. A bad plan sells the dream of delivering performance, yet it omits to mention the realities of the nightmares.

You can recognise a bad plan from the get-go because it's never about the customer, it's always about the network adviser and the money. Bad advisers may only be interested in how much money you have to invest, not why you want to invest. The assumption is always that the dream is about making money, and not that making money is a means to fulfil the dream.

Any financial planner worth their salt won't even talk about money until they properly understand you (the client), what you want to achieve with your life and (crucially) who else you are responsible for, which is where my CLEARER™ model comes into its own. Until an adviser is fully up to speed with all your goals, dreams and aspirations they haven't earned the right to talk to you about your money. Unfortunately, many people are unable to determine well enough when a bad plan lands in front of them. I don't blame them; the world of investments can seem like an alien world teeming with figures and jargon. I understand why people believe promises that sadly turn out to be false, or at best disappointing. It must be so alluring when a fund manager lays out the prospect of making big returns and even provides 'evidence' to 'prove' it (albeit based on extremely short-term results or in clever marketing around the numbers).

CASE STUDY: SUSAN

Susan, aged 56, had investments worth £640,000, actively managed by a large network, a lot of which was with a discretionary fund manager (DFM). She was concerned about the level of fees and what appeared to be very little return on her investments. Her portfolio included £326,000 in a pension; the balance was in a general investment account and an ISA.

When I looked through the file, I saw no strategy behind the management. It was as if her adviser had thrown a whole bunch of funds into the air, picked the first that landed and sold them to her in the name of 'diversification'.

The arrangements were completely disjointed, spread across thirty-nine different funds and managers; the pension was spread across seven and the DFM element included another thirty-two. How the adviser or DFM could work with so many was beyond me. An adviser's job is to select a number of good money managers, who are specialists in their fields, and who can execute a clearly defined investing model to help deliver a client's financial plan over the term the client specifies.

It was clear to me that someone had been looking through a rear-view mirror at funds and managers that had been given high ratings or stars by the industry. Susan wasn't investing in the past – she was investing for her future. The funds had very little exposure to two equity asset classes that have delivered premium index returns during the last sixty-five years in the UK, globally and in the emerging world: the small-cap and value-cap markets. Those asset classes do deliver premiums, and feature throughout my own model. Assets were allocated around 50/50 to equity and fixed income holdings but it would be near impossible to keep tabs on what was going on in the portfolio as a whole.

A cynic would say this was by design: perhaps the adviser wanted Susan to think, 'This can only be managed by someone very clever who knows what they are doing so I will hand over all responsibility and pay them the 3% per year they want from me.'

Her money was in funds that claimed to be tracking indexes but were underperforming those indexes, and by a stretch in some cases; and she was paying for active, not passive, management.

I am not a fan of flexible fixed income/equity set-ups. I know they are common, and I understand the logic, but ultimately you want the manager to believe in one or the other and manage accordingly. These balanced bond/equity set-ups can allow the manager to hold between 40% and 80% of the fund in equities, for example. Some might say that such a wide range suggests the manager of the fund can't make up their mind what to invest in. Susan's pension held a number of these bond/equity funds, all with different ratios, which made it even more difficult to grasp the overall weighting to either asset class.

There was no clear goal or firm plan embedded in her strategy. And it was limited in its equity exposure which in my professional opinion for a client of her age was unjustified.

There was more not to like. In the DFM element she also had fifty-one direct equity holdings across nine sectors. Why nine? Why fifty-one? And why would you hold fifty-one companies' shares directly in any event, if you were then going to buy and hold the same shares again through collective funds?

Clearly, that's all now been put right. And Susan's savings by shifting over to my management show as around £4,600 per annum. Naturally in year 1 the saving is £4,600 – enough on its own, some would say. But over thirty years I estimate that the saving in fees alone would have increased the value of her portfolio by around £320,000.

My plan immediately saved Susan almost 2% per year in costs and fees, which when compounded over thirty years puts a staggering amount of money back into her estate and out of the pockets of the glossy network who were lapping it up. That 2% is a huge number when it's viewed from this perspective.

7

Have You Made the Wrong Plan?

The wrong plan is commonly underpinned by a false sense of security and mostly a fear of holding equities because they present too great a risk. Only when you adopt a 360° perspective of market activity and recalibrate your relationship to investment and market risk is it possible to rebalance your portfolio of investments to outpace inflation and deliver the reassurance and returns needed to get you through a thirty-year retirement. One of the most important things anyone wants from a retirement plan is to feel reassured by the confidence that it will deliver an income through the passage of time, no matter what happens in the world around us.

From the cautious perspective, 'fixed income' and 'security' sound like good words. It should follow that a fixed income plan ticks all the boxes, certainly for the nervous, or those who like to know exactly what they will receive. In one respect, I'd agree. But it ticks the 'wrong plan' box.

Fixed income might sound good on paper but it's an income that shrinks *in real terms*, when adjusted against inflation, as you head through retirement. A fixed income strategy will certainly deliver what you expect, but it will never deliver what you need. Since the 1960s, the typical returns from fixed income securities (gilts and bonds) have been approximately 5% per annum. But the key differentiator in a fixed income strategy with a 5% return is that this figure has an attacker that eats away at its base, a parasite, with devastating consequences. That parasite is inflation, which has also run at an average of 5% over the same period.

Thus, historically, market returns from fixed income have been wiped out by inflation, which is bad news for anyone who has relied on fixed income to deliver their retirement strategy. No growth, a fund that, at best, stands still and often loses real value when adjusted against inflation. Imagine combining this with a bad plan – plus those excessive fees on top. It's happening out there every day of the week.

Generally speaking, people investing in fixed income will stand still. In effect, they will flat-line, financially. In a hospital, flat-lining means you're as good as dead. Anyone who tells you that fixed income provides reas-surance in retirement is not living in the real world.

I know of advisers who take new pension business and just agree when their client tells them they
need to be certain the fund won't fall in value. Some
advisers will smile, agree with the person in front of
them and take the business. I can't help a client who
won't accept a challenge to their views, and I tell them
so. Part of our job, or rather our calling, is to have the
difficult conversations.

Living costs have risen over the past thirty years and
without any doubt will continue to rise over the next.
What you buy today for £5 will cost upwards of £12.50
thirty years from now, if inflation continues to average
what it has over the past six decades. Investing in
fixed income renders it impossible to keep pace with
the rising cost of living.

Cash kept at the bank or building society will suffer
the same fate, if not worse, because deposit interest
rates rarely keep up with inflation. Your money will
simply lose its purchasing power. You have absolutely
no chance on this earth of getting through a retirement
of any length if you are not exposed to equities. We
can see how the items and pastimes we pay for have
moved in just the last decade, when the government
aimed to keep inflation at 2% a year.

Anyone who believes that inflation is actually running
at 2% should pause and think. In reality inflation has
always felt higher than what the government would
have us believe, because individuals rarely buy
exactly the same items, at exactly the same times, as

the 'basket of notional goods' that governments use to calculate the official inflation rate. This chart shows a number of examples.

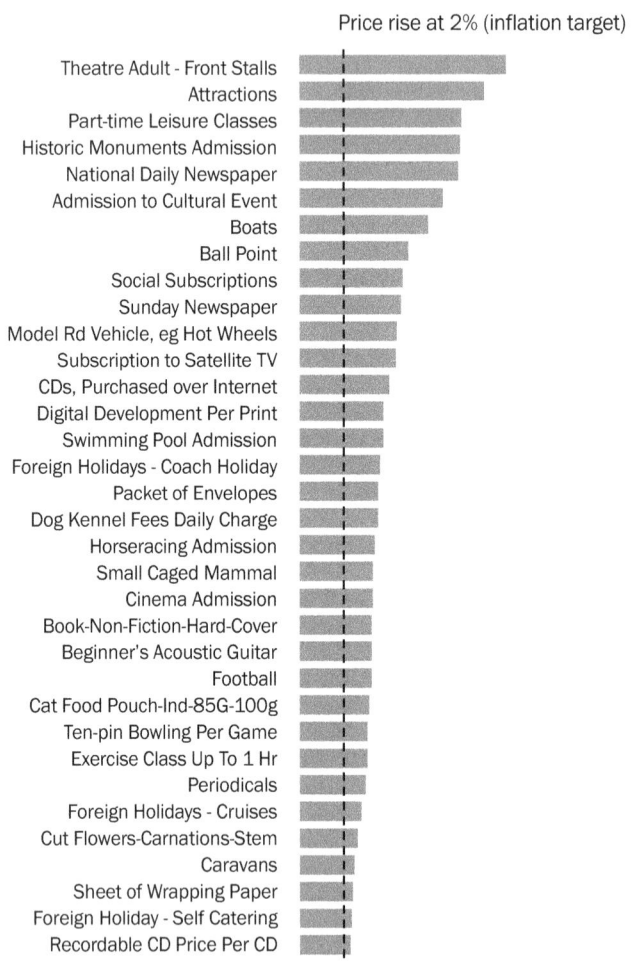

Figure 9 How prices changed between 2010 and 2019

It is worth examining three scenarios that result in people being over-reliant on fixed income strategies.

Lifestyling

Lifestyling is an internal mechanism in many pension plans that automatically and incrementally reduces holdings in equities as retirement approaches. To make this change, the pension provider increases the fixed income holdings each year (often, but not always, by investing future income in fixed income funds or securities). Thus, the percentage in equities decreases and the fixed income share increases. And this dynamic continues as you go forwards.

The rationale is purely defensive. Fixed income assets, as the name suggests, remain stable and are not as variable as equities – their prices do not move around as much. When equity markets decline (as they regularly do), fixed income assets aren't necessarily affected, or at least, not in the same way. Also, annuity prices are calculated by reference to bond/gilt yields so, the theory goes, having your money in fixed income investments should mean that its value changes in the same way, at the same time, as annuity rates.

It's supposed to be 'safer', whatever that means, and prevent people from worrying that they're still investing in stock markets. A cynic might say it's to get them to stay put when the equity markets do tank, so the pension provider can keep their income dripping in.

The word 'safe', however, is misleading. Taking into account inflation and fees, there's no discernible gain, only a loss in real terms when the pension fails to keep pace with inflation. The only peace of mind that's available is reserved for the pension provider, which won't be bombarded by angry and anxious customers when the equity markets inevitably fall.

Try taking your family on holiday, going to watch the football, or even going out for dinner with a fixed income strategy built into your later-life pension arrangement.

In my opinion, lifestyling is a disservice to all retirees of the past and future. People should be exposed as much as possible to equities before and after retirement. Equities are the only way to ensure a rise in income, despite the temporary price changes. The nervous investor who sees fixed income as a guarantee either believes that to be true, or has been persuaded that a fall in the markets is Armageddon. It's not. I cannot emphasise enough that equity markets have always recovered eventually, and once they do they continue to grow. My clear message is that people will not get through their retirement if they rely on fixed income investments.

The 'safe' option

Promoting fixed income investments within an ISA, a general investment account or a pension can be an easy sell for a financial or investment adviser. I'd actually describe it as a lazy sell, since they know the average person will probably understand little (quite often nothing) about the equity and fixed income markets.

What customers think they 'know' is often based on false assumptions, often built from past experiences of family and friends who 'lost' their pension when equity markets fell. Many people know (or have heard of) someone who lost everything in this bubble or that bubble.

Recently I took on a new client, Richard, who had around £400,000 invested in tech stocks when the tech market burst twenty years ago. His adviser sold his holdings. I worked out that Richard would have just under £1 million today if he had simply hung on to his shares. It's less often the markets that do damage, than people panicking. And quite often it's the adviser.

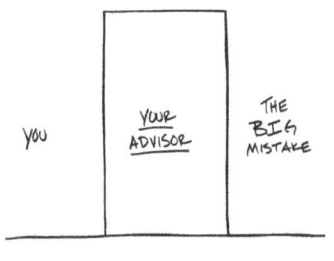

Illustration used under license from Behaviorgap.com.

Some see an adviser who recommends equity invest-ment as 'playing the markets' with their future pension money: that must inherently be dangerous. I agree that it would be if the adviser was inclined to 'play the markets'. Anything that seems 'safe' in comparison to an adviser 'playing with your money' must be the better option. Fixed income seems an easy answer, and it works because the adviser's client believes that the sum they are investing will never fall in value. But, as we have seen, the real value does drop. If only advisers would explore all the options in detail and take more time to listen to, and understand, their clients' concerns and needs. Rather than having a challenging conversation, and clearly explaining that the perceived risks may never come to pass, advisers perpetuate the myths that fixed income investments guarantee safety and certainty.

The adviser risks nothing, signs up the client and still makes their annual fee. It works for a few years, but the fund falls in real value. If the investor panics as retirement draws closer, and moves to an active adviser promising 20% annual returns to get back on track, real damage can be done. I understand that most investors are naturally cautious, especially when tackling concerns outside their own expertise for the first time. That's why it's vital that the advice that people like me give is offered in the round and supported by evidence. It's our job to reassure clients by being totally honest and transparent, not by fuel-ling their fears.

Once I can allay someone's anxieties about market volatility and show its innate ability to recover following a fall, they are more willing to recalibrate their attitude towards risk. Moments of market crisis are actually key drivers for investment success. When markets fall by 20%, my advice is to take advantage of low prices and to invest as heavily as you can with your cash buffer reserve account because the evidence shows equity markets recover, stronger. But don't try to pick stocks: invest in the market as a whole using passive index funds (see Chapter Four). What matters most is knowing how much of your portfolio is equity-based and what action to take when that portion appears to drop in value. It's the only way of making your money insure your future.

Risk tests

The psychometric risk test is standard practice. It is designed to help advisers determine a client's attitude by examining their responses to various questions about risk. If somebody scores 5 out of 10 this 'tells' an adviser that the client needs 50% in fixed income, 50% in equities. Similarly, if they score 3 out of 10, the advice is to invest 70% into fixed income and 30% into equity.

I question the value of these tests. I find them amateur. They do not accommodate any real understanding of a person's future needs and have little to do with what's best for the individual investor and their money. They ignore the most important question which is always 'How much do you need to live through retirement?' That is what should drive the balance of your investments. In compliance terms, however, the adviser must carry out the risk assessment, tick the box that supports the advice they've given, and it's signed off.

Of course, I still risk-test my clients, but the difference is that, even if they score 3 out of 10 on appetite for risk, that doesn't change my advice; I still suggest what level of equity exposure they need based on how much their lifestyle will cost them in retirement. It's my job to do the hard work, to educate my client and show them that they have little chance of being able to do all the nice things they have outlined if they don't invest for growth. They may score as naturally cautious but their real future needs usually suggest they need an equity-weighted solution.

What my risk assessment test tells me, and it does this very well, is which clients I need to reassure next time the markets drop, because the more risk-averse clients are the most scared and they need to hear me explain what's going on, and to remind them of our earlier conversations and my advice to sit tight and not to panic. Once I've explained that a drop in the market need not mean they've lost any money, and that it's simply a paper value that has temporarily dropped, that alleviates their natural anxiety. I remind them that I forewarned them this would happen and that it has already been factored into their plan.

It may well be that I recommend that they cease drawing income from the plan, temporarily; or maybe I don't. It depends on how we have created the plan. The investor might need to draw down on the cash reserves that we arranged to be held as a buffer, and invest more in equities while prices are low, in order to reap the rewards when the market eventually bounces back. These are the nitty-gritty conversations I know I need to have with clients; if I shirk doing this I am doing them and their retirement a disservice.

Having that kind of relationship with customers wasn't possible when I worked for the big institutions. If you work for a large bank or investment house you have to toe the employer's line. If the institution has 1,500 or 3,000 advisers it can't let them all run such a bespoke strategy. Hence the risk test. Is it a way of driving the herd to conform? I would say most definitely.

The wrong plan, therefore, is contingent on any or all of the above, but in my opinion, the wrong plan presents the biggest problem to investors. On paper it may seem to sensibly take them down the right path by addressing any concerns about risk, but it's still the wrong plan. In all probability, clients will end up with a portfolio too heavily weighted to fixed income, that will ultimately fail to outpace inflation, thus seeing its value eroded in real terms. The portfolio's purchasing power will simply diminish.

The key to reaching the right balance in a portfolio between fixed income and equities shouldn't be based on a fear of risk. It should be based on the clear understanding that this context is actually the gyration of equity prices. And whilst equity prices fluctuate in the past the falls have always been temporary, and in the long term the market as a whole has constantly increased upwards.

If we viewed risk through a different lens, as actual goods in the shops, we'd have a better relationship with it. For example, if the price of my favourite canned tuna fillets drops one week by, say, 25%, I know it will eventually climb back up. I also know that, in the not-too-distant future, they will be more expensive to buy than they were last week. Using spare capital to buy that tuna in bulk at today's low price (forty or fifty cans, say, depending on how long I think the tuna will stay fresh) would be a shrewd move because when the price eventually increases again I will have saved a lot of money. Shouldn't we be thinking about our investments and pensions in the same way?

Global stock markets always move up and down but over time they grow. What you see in between the growth is the gyration of prices. The big mistake people often make is confusing risk with gyration.

Risk is all in our heads: the risk is that we might lose money, but it only becomes real and permanent damage if we panic and cash the pension in at the bottom of the market. Planning for these fluctuations should give you the confidence to wait them out.

CASE STUDY: DARREN

Darren had a plan. The wrong plan.

At 48 he had a pension with a well-known insurance company. It was 100% invested into fixed income investments, yielding a lower-than-average 2% per annum. When I asked why he had committed his entire pension fund to fixed income his explanation was that he was scared of losing money if he invested in equity markets. He had transferred out of equities and into fixed income after a previous market decline had spooked him.

He was afraid of looking at his portfolio online (which he did every day) and seeing that his £160,000 had dropped to £120,000. In his mind that would have been a £40,000 loss. He'd chosen fixed income investments so that he could log on and be reassured that his £160,000 was still worth £160,000.

Darren intuitively knew that his fixed income plan would never deliver the returns he'd really need in retirement, but he simply couldn't see himself being comfortable with anything else. His fear of market volatility was holding him back.

I asked him what his ideal retirement lifestyle looked like and we spoke of travel and other family-linked bits and pieces that all added up to an estimated future income need. I explained that unless he was prepared to change his plan, he would have no chance of securing anything close to the income he would need, unless he was prepared to expose himself to global equities in the knowledge that periodically the value of his investments might drop.

I presented him with the evidence in Figure 4 showing nearly seven decades of fixed income returns using UK one-month Treasury bills as an example, along with the real returns with inflation factored in. We then looked at the contrasting returns from equities. We explored the numbers together and looked deep into the historic temporary falls and declines in global equity market indices including our UK FTSE 100 and the US Dow.

Darren started to see for himself how falling markets had always bounced back stronger over time. He started to feel more comfortable with equities and when it came to the crunch I didn't have to convince him of anything. I simply asked him to tell me, based on the evidence that I had put in front of him, what level of exposure to equities he could live with. He replied 60%.

I felt he could probably go a bit higher, but he was heading in the right direction. He did score low on a risk test, and somebody at a network would have had to put him 60% into fixed income. Despite his

Table 6 Equity and fixed income investments

EQUITY	0%	20%	40%	60%	80%	100%
FIXED INCOME	100%	80%	60%	40%	20%	0%
One-Year Total Return (%)	1.59	6.3	10.1	14.22	18.44	20.88
Three-Year Total Return (%)	0.43	2.59	4.3	6.08	7.85	8.85
Five-Year Total Return (%)	0.98	3.57	5.8	8.11	10.41	12.1
Ten-Year Total Return (%)	2.31	4.65	6.57	8.53	10.48	11.73
Fifteen-Year Total Return (%)	3.47	5.31	6.81	8.3	9.72	10.69
Twenty-Year Total Return (%)	4.47	5.67	6.53	7.35	8.08	8.36
Annualised Return (%) 1990–2019	6.81	7.48	7.98	8.44	8.8	8.86
Annualised Standard Deviation (%) 1990–2019	2.78	3.48	6.04	8.93	11.89	14.66
Lowest One-Year Return (%)	-2.16 09/17 to 08/18	-1.87 02/94 to 01/95	-9.40 11/07 to 10/08	-16.56 11/07 to 10/08	-24.11 01/90 to 12/90	-32.06 01/90 to 12/90
Lowest Annualised Three-Year Return (%)	-0.30 07/10 to 06/19	2.25 11/16 to 10/19	0.07 03/06 to 02/09	-3.22 03/06 to 02/09	-6.81 04/00 to 03/03	-10.81 04/00 to 03/03
Highest One-Year Return (%)	21.85 01/91 to 12/91	22.96 10/90 to 09/91	32.36 09/92 to 08/93	43.22 09/92 to 08/93	54.82 09/92 to 08/93	66.69 09/92 to 08/93
Highest Annualised Three-Year Return (%)	19.26 05/90 to 04/93	18.71 10/90 to 09/93	19.89 10/90 to 09/93	21.08 10/90 to 09/93	22.24 04/03 to 03/06	26.37 04/03 to 03/06
Growth of £1 1990–2019	7.22	8.7	10.01	11.38	12.57	12.77

risk test score, I would have been comfortable with recommending 70% weighted to equity. I know that I will need to reassure him when the next inevitable drop hits us, as they do every five or seven years. The various numbers in Table 6 show how the nineteen years to December 2019 played out. The 60% equity model can be seen alongside the pure fixed income model, like the one Darren had at the start of our discussion.

It was touch and go as to whether Darren and I would work together. What I had to say was not what he intuitively wanted to hear, but it was what he needed to hear. His previous financial advisers had reinforced his perceptions surrounding market risk. They didn't question him further or offer alternative approaches, they simply pandered to his anxiety and sold him an insurance company pension product to match that fear. His actual needs to see him through his retirement never came into the discussion.

In the middle of the 2020 pandemic, equity markets were generally 20% down from previous highs. Darren began to sell down small amounts of his remaining fixed income holdings and gradually increased his equity holdings.

8

... And Breathe

What is helpful for us all, regardless of where we sit on the 'risk' scale, is not just the long-term performance of equities but, probably even more importantly, the lowest one-year and three-year returns. Table 6 shows that the more equity you hold the sharper the temporary declines. Nobody enjoys opening their account online and seeing their money 32% down. I'm no different – I don't like it either. But note: this is not real damage. It is simply price gyration. Like the tuna.

When it comes to investing, we can be our own worst enemy if we don't manage our behaviour. It's important to accept that the benefits of equity investing are realised over a period of time, not overnight.

There's a price to pay with everything in life, and the price you pay here (for an income underpinned by global equities, which you probably will not outlive) is acceptance that sometimes there will be a temporary reduction in prices that may see your nice £250,000 pension appear to have 'lost' £75,000 every five years or so. It's only a loss if you sell when the prices are low. Remember the tuna. Buy more of it and definitely stock up on it if your financial plan suggests this is needed in order to maintain your lifestyle throughout retirement.

Thousands of hard-working people are regularly exposed to misleading media articles that prey on their fears of loss. For example, in March 2018 it was widely reported that Facebook's Mark Zuckerberg lost £40 billion in a single day. Zuckerberg only faced a temporary revaluation of his shareholdings and I very much doubt if he was seriously bothered. Nor will he have sold any of his holdings in response. In fact, over the following twelve months Facebook's share price recovered and grew to its highest level ever. However, stories like that feed the fear for people like Darren.

This is when clients need to be able to turn to a solid financial adviser as their sounding board and emergency service, who can tell them the world is not ending and to stay calm. It's our role to help preserve our clients' sanity when the media is kicking up a storm all around us. Which they always do. Always remember what NEWS stands for: Negative Events

World Service. My advice? Turn it off. All of it. Please try to see past the temporary declines in stock prices and ignore the noise. If your portfolio is set up and diversified properly, and if you have an enlightened investment adviser to keep you calm (and stop you committing horrendous and often irreparable self-harm at these critical junctions), you will be ok. The recovery typically always gathers pace soon after a drop, and ultimately the advance continues on its path to new heights. Clients need reassurance that their investments will continue to support their plan, into which price gyrations have already been factored, and that they'll be OK. We're their wingman.

Retirement was once referred to as the 'golden years' but is now a much more complex picture, as we saw in Part One. Above and beyond the financial crisis of 2008, the way in which money has been saved and invested for retirement has been flawed, meaning that for ordinary people retirement is likely to be a struggle, despite the fact that many have been prudent and careful savers.

Therefore, we all need to change our perceptions about how we save, how we address the myth of risk and how we plan our financial affairs. Never before has the 'no plan'/'bad plan'/'wrong plan' question needed the attention it now warrants.

The paradox alongside of all that is that the financial industry, as a whole, has never paid its advisers to do the deep thinking and planning that clients need. Instead, even today some financial products are sold on commission. Advisers are encouraged to sell certain provider products. In the big insurance companies an adviser can earn huge commissions – nothing like the maximum cover plans from the 1980s and 1990s, but they run on the same fuel.

As a result, clients who engage advisers from the bigger institutions may find they are never encouraged to even think about the big questions we have touched on. The focus will be on products: investments, insurance and pensions. My belief is that this has contributed to a situation where potential clients just switch off and do nothing because the advice does not relate to their plans, dreams and life goals. Such a shame given the number of decent advisers, with a heart and a head, who I know are out there.

When a new potential client first walks through my door, they generally already have a gut feeling that they may have a problem with their pension, or an investment, or perhaps an estate planning issue that needs solving. However, before we even begin to discuss finance, I often discover that they don't have any real plan in place, or if they do, it can feel cobbled together, unclear or possibly even unsuitable.

With that in mind, I create a complete picture that provides me with deep insights into their background and current life, their goals, dreams, and aspirations.

This forms a foundation from which I can begin to know them better, and helps them feel secure and confident that I have their interests at heart. It's only then that it's really possible to tune into how I might be able to support them with their financial planning.

When I investigate a potential new client's current position, I often find they have been dealing with an adviser with no belief system. You will have gathered by now that I have a strong belief system, which is summarised in the Wilcocks & Wilcocks ten-point investment plan. These are the key messages we convey to clients (and anyone else who's listening): our ten golden rules for making investments work, and for avoiding the no plan/bad plan/wrong plan scenarios.

The ten-point investment plan

1. We are investment advisers, not investment forecasters, speculators or crystal ball readers. We don't believe anybody can successfully predict investment markets or returns continuously, nor will they ever be able to outperform equity markets on a consistent and repeatable basis.

2. Exposure to the entire developed world and emerging world equity markets, as opposed to fixed income markets – even during retirement years – is a must. Get this one thing right on its

own, and we stand a chance of seeing our money outlive us. Get it wrong, and we will most likely outlive the money.

3. Fixed income as an asset class used to work in the 1970s and 1980s when people tended to retire at 65 and live until 75. Nowadays, it'll never get us through a three-decade retirement, and if relying on fixed income to get us through retirement, we will, in Wilcocks & Wilcocks' opinion, outlive our money.

4. Small-cap equity and value-cap equity exposure, alongside main market large-cap equity exposure, again diversified across the entire developed and emerging world, will continue to be essential to give us exposure to higher expected returns over time.

5. We trust the various equity markets we deploy to do their work, and all the evidence I have found points towards this combined strategy winning over pure 'actively managed' alternatives that are found to fail in over 80% of cases (see Chapter Two).

6. Crucially, having exposure to all groups and classes of equities across both the developed and the emerging world gives you the broad asset, sector and geographic diversification to capture returns from all markets.

7. Keeping overall costs to *circa* 1.6% per annum so that the drag on investment growth is relatively

low is also important. By way of example, a 1% additional fee on a starting fund of £250,000 (whatever vehicle it's in) would see fees totalling £250,000 taken from the portfolio over a thirty-year retirement, if inflation continues at 2.5% and equities earn 5.5%.

8. Keeping calm and not selling out when the markets fall, as they regularly do, and always will. When everyone else's behaviour is, or appears, erratic, you must stay calm because the falls have always been temporary and long-term market growth outpaces them. Do not 'throw the portfolio overboard'. Ever.

9. In fact, where others panic, you should double up on regular contributions or invest further capital into our globally diversified equity model when the markets do tank, as much as possible, to buy in whilst prices are low. And because you will be buying when prices are low, you may even beat the fund managers we recommend at their own game.

10. In our opinion, that's pretty much all it takes to make and then keep people wealthy. It's then a case of managing behaviour, and safe income withdrawal to support retirement income needs as the years unfold, whilst managing the portfolio and plan alongside inflation and keeping the faith in what we started.

PART FOUR

THE SOLUTION: CLEARER™

9

C for Clarity

One of the best things about being an independent financial adviser with the freedom to run the practice in my own way is the opportunity to create unique relationships with my clients that aren't mapped out by compliance officers or governed by sales targets and silly rules. My previous experiences in the hard-nosed, sales-oriented world of large institutions hadn't sufficiently prepared me to create such relationships.

Asking the right questions

Over the years, we have invested in our training and development with the client at the centre of our ideology and aim, honing our listening skills and learning how to engage clients by asking simple, searching questions.

I'm not a huge fan of old-style fact-finding question-naires that mine for data and bore the socks off poten-tial new customers. So, for prospective clients plan-ning their retirement, we often start with the three questions below. They always get people thinking in a way that most will not have thought before.

The point behind these challenging questions is to make us think about what we really want out of life. The aim is to help clients identify and then go on and achieve their ideal lifestyle. Set out like this, a plan begins to fall into place, often for the first time, and the 'magic number' they've never thought about can become clear. Our planning at this point has a focus.

Try the exercise yourself below, noting your answers on a separate piece of paper. You can also download a free copy of the complete financial planning question-naire template at www.martinwilcocks.co.uk/flp.

FINANCIAL PLANNING QUESTIONNAIRE

Question 1

I want you to imagine that you are financially secure, that you have enough money to take care of your needs, now and in the future. Ask yourself: How would I live my life? Would I change anything?

Let yourself go. Don't hold back on your dreams. Describe a life that is complete, that is richly yours.

Question 2

Having recently visited your doctor, you were told that you have only five or ten years left to live. The good part is that you won't ever feel sick. The bad news is that you will have no notice of the moment of your death. What will you do in the time you have remaining to live? Will you change your life, and how will you do it?

Question 3

This time your doctor shocks you with the news that you have only one day left to live. Notice what feelings arise as you confront your very real mortality. Ask yourself: What did I miss? Who did I not get to be? What did I not get to do?

This material was developed by George Kinder and Kinder Institute of Life Planning. It is part of a training program that leads to the Registered Life Planner® designation. Used by permission of George Kinder © 1999-2020.

Digging deeper

For some people, this initial session comes as a complete, yet welcome, surprise, especially if they've already been exposed to a glossy network. They may not be used to someone listening to them with intent, and it may be the first time they have articulated their hopes and dreams to a trustworthy adviser.

Once the conversation is flowing and the topics that come out of that probing session are up for discussion it sometimes turns out that the person I'm talking to may not be completely happy with their life as it stands, and for some it's high time to make some adjustments, subtle or otherwise.

I keep the planning simple. At the end of the day everything you want to be, or have, that isn't in place already, comes from the three questions. If you haven't felt able to answer, I suggest shutting yourself away to think. Or even book a weekend away by yourself, somewhere quiet with a view.

Once the penny drops and you can envisage what you want, I let a second layer of questions flow:

1. 'What's stopping you?' And I will remain silent until the answers come back – even if the silence lasts for ten minutes, which it can.

2. 'When shall we start to kick over those hurdles?' For some people, talking this stage through takes an hour; for others, a single minute.

3. 'When will we be done with the transition, with you complete as a person?' We can talk about this for as long as it takes to put a sensible timeline down on paper.

Result

And when the answers are there in front of us, I suggest we try to write them all down on one page of A4 paper. If it goes over one page, it's too complicated. Too much detail is the killer of dreams. People get caught up in intricacies that have the potential to make a tiny difference, and progress stops. You will fine-tune once the plan is working. And then it's my job to chase progress. I follow a three-part rule:

1. **Dream:** Write down everything – why you must, how you will and when.

2. **Action:** Get on with it – no excuses, no faffing, taking no prisoners.

3. **Mentor:** Someone holding you to account on agreed outputs, on agreed dates.

Using the following chart, think about your 'GOALS' using the questions as a starting point. Write your answers to these questions and keep them to refer to.

DREAM	GOAL	Why is this important?
		How will you feel when you have achieved this?
		What effect could it have on the people around you?
ACTION	OBSTACLES	Why has it taken you until now to start this?
		What barriers needed moving out of your way?
		When will you be clear to focus?
	ACTION	What do you need to do right now?
		What is one huge step forward you could implement today?
		What would you do after that?
	LEARN	How will you keep motivated and stick to this plan?
		When will you achieve this goal?
		What would failure to meet the goal feel like?
MENTOR	SUPPORT	Who can you speak with to help you stay on track?
		Will that person check in with you every two weeks?
		What other external support might be necessary?

10

L for Lifestyle Financial Planning

How much money do you need to achieve and maintain that dream lifestyle?

If you are living the dream already, great. We can skip to the financial plan that will secure your lifestyle throughout your retirement years. When we know what your ideal life looks like, and how much it will cost, we then need to consider what financial resources we have around us now and whether they will do the job of carrying you and your family through the passage of time.

If they are insufficient, we will need to think about what we will actually need, and when we will need it and for how long. This involves looking forward in time and is based on a number of assumptions and expectations all built around the life goals we are working to.

Table 7 Current assumptions in my financial planning software

Inflation (UK Retail Price Index)		2.5%
Cash returns		1.0%
Fixed income portfolio		2.0%
Equity portfolio	50%	5.0%
	70%	6.0%
	90%	7.0%
Property returns		7.0%

What's your number?

The key exercise is to run through an expenditure analysis that breaks down what your ideal lifestyle costs from an ideal retirement age, which may be 60, to the point at which you slow down and take a back seat at perhaps 80; from that point onwards expenditure might drop off until 90; and then nudge down again. Or maybe expenditure goes up because you want to move into that fabulous retirement facility down the road, as opposed to local authority sheltered housing. It's all up for debate. Here is a short exercise to get you tuned into that what that dream lifestyle might cost. Try working out your own numbers:

Table 8 Expenditure recorder

Expenditure classes	Current Lifestyle	Stage 1 (enter ages) (___ to ___)	Stage 2 (___ to ___)	Stage 3 (___ to ___)
Property				
Food				
Bills				
Dining out				
Holidays				
Travel				
Children				
Clothes				
Charity				
Cars				
Clubs				
Other				
Totals				

Once we know the magic numbers, we can then work out a target fund and create an investment plan that also factors in envisaged inflation. A more detailed expenditure exercise can be downloaded at www. martinwilcocks.co.uk/exp.

11

E for Evidence-Based Investing

Around ten years ago Rob (my brother and business partner) and I were exploring how we might improve our investing strategy. There is so much noise in the world of financial advising and planning, and it comes at you from so many angles.

Rob came across Dimensional Fund Advisors at an event in 2011. They encourage advisers to explore investment management in depth from an academic perspective. These encounters sparked in us a new sense of purpose and responsibility, rooted in proper market data and analysis as opposed to talking up the latest fund. We realised this was the way forward with our clients: in providing them with real information and what they need to know and, more importantly, understand.

From that point forward, our business began to grow. Our eyes were opened to trusting the market as a friend and not as a volatile psychopath. We could see the benefits from investing in all classes of global equities but in particular small-cap and value-cap variants that had delivered higher returns over the course of time that made a real difference.

As an investment strategy, it's both proven and viable because it's backed by an abundance of independent and peer-reviewed evidence. Each sector will rise and fall, or ebb and flow, at different times, but the fact that a portfolio is exposed across the board means that it has sufficient elasticity at all times to support and keep the investment afloat. And on the back of that you won't experience 'faulty reasoning syndrome' that keeps lots of people awake all night.

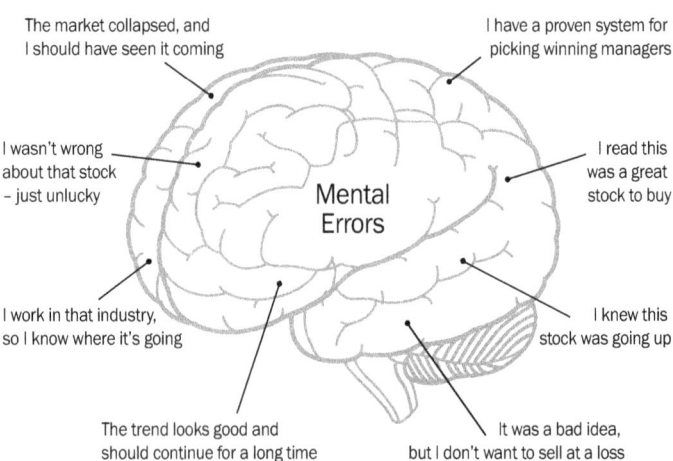

Figure 10 Humans are not wired for disciplined investing: when people follow their natural instincts, they tend to apply faulty reasoning to investing

With the help of Dimensional we redrew our investment business model. It couldn't be more unlike the preposterous claims of active investment managers who base their entire proposition on speculating with clients' money in the hope of winning the jackpot if they're lucky, by beating the market. The evidence shows that this type of luck doesn't repeat itself and seldom occurs in the first place. It's not a belief system, it's a fallacy lacking foundation and vacillates between having no plan, a bad plan and a wrong plan, all rolled into one.

We point clients toward academic data that proves diversification across all sectors is the only guaranteed way that their money will grow over time and provide them with the lifestyle they wish to achieve. Compliance officers will of course start to shake when they see the word I have just used – 'guarantee' – but in reality, diversification is the only way their money will grow sustainably. Just look at the data.

Assets vs inflation

Let's recap the main investment sectors:

- Cash (bank and building society accounts)
- Fixed income (bonds and gilts)
- Equities (stocks and shares)
- Property

Cash and Fixed Income

Since 1956 the average rate of return from a savings account has been approximately 5% and fixed income securities, bonds and gilts have provided around the same.

Equites

The index return from developed world stock markets has averaged around 10% per annum over any long period. Interestingly, small-cap and value-cap stock markets have achieved returns of around 14% per annum. For a closer look, Table 8 compares the index returns from several major stock indices, some of which we summarised earlier in Figure 4.

Property

Property investment returns typically average 7% per annum, although this very much depends upon the asset itself (residential or commercial) and nature of stake (privately owned or a share in a property fund). If you buy property as an investment, you need to buy the physical asset, which means legal fees, valuation costs and stamp duty. You then have to put a tenant in, possibly with a paid letting agent in support, who will charge around 15%. After that, you might be lucky with the tenant and have nice people who look after things and pay the rent on time; or you might not. Then there's the roof, the boiler, the utilities and the windows.

Why bother, when I can get net returns from property, and avoid all the headaches, by simply investing in a global property fund? It's exposed to the same physical assets, and instead of my owning bricks and mortar in, say, Liverpool, I own a tiny part of thousands of properties, in a variety of different sectors globally. Which in turn, just like our equity model, reduces what people perceive to be risk (price gyration, as you now know it).

Inflation

We have talked about the enemy, inflation. Since the mid-1950s it's averaged out at around 5% per year. We saw in the Darren case study that in the thirty years from 1990 to 2019 it had been 2.9% per year. I suspect we may see this rise over time as our cycles continue to spin. If you compare rates of return on cash, or fixed income, with the rate of inflation, it should be glaringly obvious that by investing in these sectors your money is likely to lose real value.

The price you pay to see your money stay about level with no day-to-day fluctuation in price is very high and is near-certain to see you lose money in real terms. Every £100,000 at the bank needs to be worth £102,500 this time next year at current rates of inflation. Will it? And as we saw earlier, try taking the children on holiday again next year, for a budget only 2.5% more than this year's.

Table 8 Annualised rates of returns (%)[9]

	1 Year	5 Years	10 Years	15 Years	20 Years
	2019	2015–2019	2010–2019	2005–2019	2000–2019
Dimensional Global Core Equity Index	22.2	12.4	12.4	10.7	8.4
Dimensional Global Large Value Index	18.8	11.0	11.3	9.0	8.2
Dimensional Global Small Index	19.6	11.5	12.6	10.9	10.7
Dimensional Global Targeted Value Index	17.5	10.5	11.7	10.5	11.7
Dimensional Emerging Markets Core Equity Index	11.5	9.3	6.9	12.0	9.9
Dimensional Emerging Markets Value Index	6.1	8.6	5.4	11.8	11.5
Dimensional Emerging Markets Small Index	10.6	9.8	7.5	12.1	10.4
Dimensional Emerging Markets Targeted Value Index	7.0	9.3	6.6	12.3	11.9
Inflation: UK Retail Price Index	2.2	2.5	3.0	2.9	2.8
UK One-Month Treasury Bills	0.7	0.4	0.4	1.6	2.4
UK One-Month Treasury Bills (Inflation Adjusted)	-1.4	-2.0	-2.5	-1.2	-0.4
FTSE World Government Bond Index (Hedged to GBP)	7.5	4.2	5.7	5.5	5.6
Dimensional UK Core Equity Index	21.6	8.5	9.2	8.6	6.7
Dimensional UK Market Index	18.6	7.5	8.1	7.7	5.0
Dimensional UK Market Index (Inflation Adjusted)	16.0	4.8	5.0	4.6	2.2
Dimensional UK Marketwide Value Index	15.0	6.6	6.9	4.0	4.7
Dimensional UK Marketwide Value Index (Inflation Adjusted)	12.6	3.9	3.8	1.0	1.8
Dimensional UK Small Cap Index	28.0	10.0	12.9	10.7	9.7
Dimensional UK Small Cap Index (Inflation Adjusted)	25.2	7.3	9.6	7.5	6.7
Dimensional International ex UK Core Equity Index	22.3	12.8	12.7	10.9	8.5
Dimensional International ex UK Large Value Index	19.1	11.1	11.5	9.3	8.4
Dimensional International ex UK Small Index	19.4	11.7	12.8	11.0	10.9
Dimensional Europe Core Equity Index	19.9	10.3	9.1	9.1	7.3
Dimensional Europe Large Value Index	13.2	8.4	6.8	6.5	5.7
Dimensional Europe Small Index	22.2	12.1	11.1	10.8	10.5
Dimensional Japan Small Cap Index	15.7	14.6	12.9	9.6	8.7
Dimensional Asia Pacific ex Japan Small Cap Index	9.4	7.8	6.5	9.0	9.5
Dimensional US Large Cap Value Index (in USD)	28.1	8.6	12.4	7.3	8.2
Dimensional US Small Cap Index (in USD)	23.3	7.8	12.4	8.7	10.1

This gives us some real home truths about what we need to achieve from investing our money, to successfully sustain us through retirement, during which time living costs could well rise perhaps three-fold. Bonds, gilts, treasury stock and corporate bonds (debt investments) are not to be relied upon to outpace inflation in the long term and so the only two asset classes that make sense are property and equities. This is where I invest my money, my family's money and my clients' money.

You must always remember that investing in equities is no 'get rich quick scheme' and long-term discipline is required. If we look at how the UK equity market has performed alongside a fixed income alternative shown below (UK one-month Treasury bills), we can see how it would have been easy to lose a little bit of faith in the fourteen years between 1960 and 1974. But balance it out over your thirty-year retirement and it's a no-brainer. Never throw the portfolio overboard. Ever.

Table 9 *The importance of long-term discipline: annualised compound returns (%)*

	1956–2019	1960–1974	1975–2019
Dimensional UK Market Index	11.81	2.91	14.15
UK One-Month Treasury Bills	6.45	6.40	6.65

Passive vs active

You will know by now that this is one of my favourite topics. To recap, passive investment involves staying put and saving as much money on fees as possible. It's also about having high levels of diversification in your portfolio, for example by investing across the UK equity market, the global equity market and the emerging world equity markets: a broad range of geographic locations and categories with large-cap, growth, small-cap and value-cap companies. And investing in every sector, as opposed just picking out healthcare or financials (for example). Evidence shows that if you just buy and hold like this, you'll be OK in the long term.

If you can strap in for the ride, you will secure the return the whole market achieves. And you can see how that would have played out for you had you invested £1 into the global equity market in 1970, closed your eyes through some of the worst stock

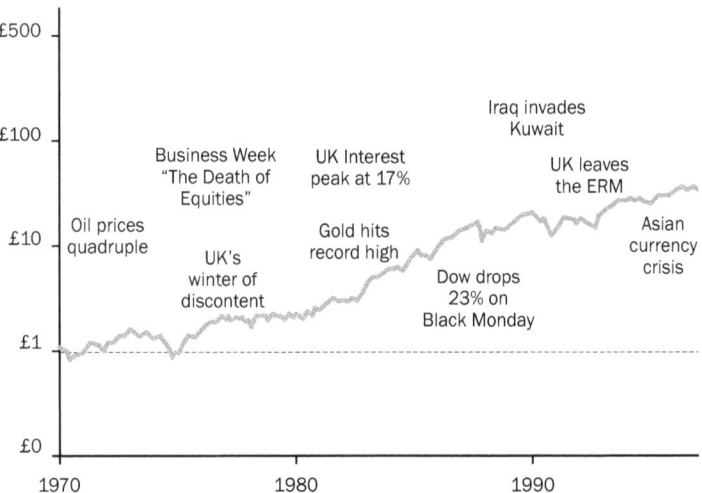

Figure 11 Markets have rewarded discipline: growth of a pound – MSCI World Index (net div), 1970–2020; a disciplined investor looks beyond the concerns of today to the long-term growth potential of markets.

Note: *Data presented in this chart is hypothetical and assumes reinvestment of income and no transaction costs or taxes. The chart is for illustrative*

market crashes in recent history and looked back in on your portfolio's progress at the end of 2020.

Cost drag

We are back to the £64 billion problem, and here is another example. Typically, a financial planning-focused investment adviser like myself will cost around 1% a year. By contrast, a typical active wealth manager who forecasts and speculates may charge

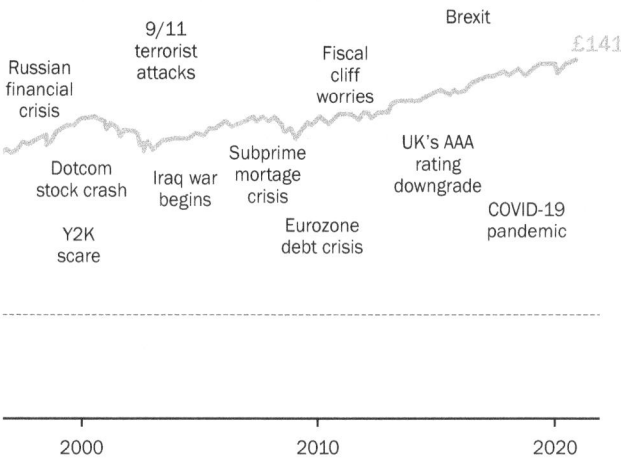

purposes only and is not indicative of any investment. Past performance (including hypothetical past performance) does not guarantee future or actual results. Performance may increase or decrease as a result of currency fluctuations. Expressed in GBP. These events are not offered to explain market returns. Instead, they serve as a reminder that investors should view daily events from a long-term perspective and avoid making investment decisions based solely on the news.

anywhere between 1% and 2% per year. Fund, product or custodian fees can add another 1%; and don't forget trading fees. An FCA study suggested that they can be very difficult to identify and in one extreme example they found transaction costs added a staggering, and please hold your breath at this point, additional 4% per year.[16] Whilst extreme, it does underline the overall point I am making. I remember reading a study that suggested on average it's an additional 0.35% per year. However, because I am now getting on a bit, and forgetful, I can't find it anywhere. It could equally be the case that I dreamt it! In any event, the quoted study paints the picture sufficiently for me to be comfortable stating that my 0.35% theory stands up. Finally, the networks can charge 5% or sometimes even 6% as initial fees. They may also lock you in for years, too (ie write into the contract or agreement financial penalties for terminating it within a specified period).

Ideally around 1.5% per year should cover adviser fees, fund fees and platform fees for passive investment and financial planning advice. If you're invested in an equity portfolio which is returning 10% per annum on average, then you are beating the current inflation rate and coming out with a solid positive return. As I mentioned earlier, you should not underestimate how much impact fees can have on your investment return over a long period. Table 10 shows how a £250,000, equity-biased portfolio may grow over thirty years with a reasonable return of 7% above

Table 10 *Illustrative growth of equity portfolio with 4% effective annual rate.*

Final investment value
£547,780.79

Initial balance
£250,000.00

Total interest earned
£297,780.79

Total monthly deposits
£0.00

Effective annual rate
4%

Year	Year Deposits	Year Interest	Total Deposits	Total Interest	Balance
1	£0.00	£10,000.00	£250,000.00	£10,000.00	£260,000.00
2	£0.00	£10,400.00	£250,000.00	£20,400.00	£270,400.00
3	£0.00	£10,816.00	£250,000.00	£31,216.00	£281,216.00
4	£0.00	£11,248.64	£250,000.00	£42,464.64	£292,464.64
5	£0.00	£11,698.59	£250,000.00	£54,163.23	£304,163.23
6	£0.00	£12,166.53	£250,000.00	£66,329.75	£316,329.75
7	£0.00	£12,653.19	£250,000.00	£78,982.94	£328,982.94
8	£0.00	£13,159.32	£250,000.00	£92,142.26	£342,142.26
9	£0.00	£13,685.69	£250,000.00	£105,827.95	£355,827.95
10	£0.00	£14,233.12	£250,000.00	£120,061.07	£370,061.07
11	£0.00	£14,802.44	£250,000.00	£134,863.51	£384,863.51
12	£0.00	£15,394.54	£250,000.00	£150,258.05	£400,258.05
13	£0.00	£16,010.32	£250,000.00	£166,268.38	£416,268.38
14	£0.00	£16,650.74	£250,000.00	£182,919.11	£432,919.11
15	£0.00	£17,316.76	£250,000.00	£200,235.88	£450,235.88
16	£0.00	£18,009.44	£250,000.00	£218,245.31	£468,245.31
17	£0.00	£18,729.81	£250,000.00	£236,975.12	£486,975.12
18	£0.00	£19,479.00	£250,000.00	£256,454.13	£506,454.13
19	£0.00	£20,258.17	£250,000.00	£276,712.29	£526,712.29
20	£0.00	£21,068.49	£250,000.00	£297,780.79	£547,780.79

Note: *Interest compounded yearly.*

Table 11 *Illustrative growth of equity portfolio with 5.5% effective annual rate.*

Final investment value
£729,439.37

Initial balance
£250,000.00

Total interest earned
£479,439.37

Total monthly deposits
£0.00

Effective annual rate
5.5%

Year	Year Deposits	Year Interest	Total Deposits	Total Interest	Balance
1	£0.00	£13,750.00	£250,000.00	£13,750.00	£263,750.00
2	£0.00	£14,506.25	£250,000.00	£28,256.25	£278,256.25
3	£0.00	£15,304.09	£250,000.00	£43,560.34	£293,560.34
4	£0.00	£16,145.82	£250,000.00	£59,706.16	£309,706.16
5	£0.00	£17,033.84	£250,000.00	£76,740.00	£326,740.00
6	£0.00	£17,970.70	£250,000.00	£94,710.70	£344,710.70
7	£0.00	£18,959.09	£250,000.00	£113,669.79	£363,669.79
8	£0.00	£20,001.84	£250,000.00	£133,671.63	£383,671.63
9	£0.00	£21,101.94	£250,000.00	£154,773.57	£404,773.57
10	£0.00	£22,262.55	£250,000.00	£177,036.11	£427,036.11
11	£0.00	£23,486.99	£250,000.00	£200,523.10	£450,523.10
12	£0.00	£24,778.77	£250,000.00	£225,301.87	£475,301.87
13	£0.00	£26,141.60	£250,000.00	£251,443.47	£501,443.47
14	£0.00	£27,579.39	£250,000.00	£279,022.87	£529,022.87
15	£0.00	£29,096.26	£250,000.00	£308,119.12	£558,119.12
16	£0.00	£30,696.55	£250,000.00	£338,815.67	£588,815.67
17	£0.00	£32,384.86	£250,000.00	£371,200.54	£621,200.54
18	£0.00	£34,166.03	£250,000.00	£405,366.57	£655,366.57
19	£0.00	£36,045.16	£250,000.00	£441,411.73	£691,411.73
20	£0.00	£38,027.65	£250,000.00	£479,439.37	£729,439.37

Note: *Interest compounded yearly.*

inflation, but with an active charging model taking 3% per annum out.

Table 11 adds back in the excess fees of 1.5%, to show the difference this makes. Over the same period, it delivers just under £182,000 more. That might just help a 44-year-old, like my client Peter who wants to retire at 60 and spend around £60,000 per year on his dream retirement. He'll probably get through to 85 without any major headaches or cause for concern. He would definitely need more than £250,000 to start with, but you get the point. Adding back just 1% per annum can have a huge impact.

Five key principles

1. We think an adviser's job is to select a small, manageable number of the best money managers, who are specialists in their fields, and who can execute a clearly defined investing strategy that helps us to deliver a client's financial plan over the longer term.

2. We are not focused on funds with stars, or superhero managers, or other glossy ratings. We aren't investing in the past, we are investing for the future. Our model is a collective fund set up and managed by just three proven fund managers, and everyone we look after has the same set-up. We invest our own capital and our families' capital in the same model.

3. The only thing that changes is the weighting of equity over fixed income in each portfolio, which depends on how cautious or aggressive the client wishes to be: cautious is 50/50, balanced 70/30 and adventurous 90/10. We decide on the bond and equity split based on risk testing, but we also use Dimensional material and data and focus on soft questions. And of course, risk isn't the same as volatility or market price gyration, and just because someone scores 5 on a risk test doesn't mean they should have 50% in fixed income.

4. We don't run hundreds of different options and variations for the 170 individual investors we currently look after as we do not believe any financial planner can manage such a dynamic. Being independent isn't about giving every one of the 170 something different. It is about being able to go where we want and choose what we think is the best route without any restrictions.

5. With the investment policy sorted, we are then free to focus on the bigger issues in financial planning for our clients, such as preserving capital throughout potentially three decades of retirement, delivering sufficient income against rising living costs, and putting plans in place to make sure surplus capital eventually passes to children, or other beneficiaries like charities or good causes close to our client's heart, safely and tax-efficiently.

Three risk portfolios

Our portfolios are operated using three different investment approaches:

- Cautious

- Balanced

- Adventurous

Cautious

Of the portfolio, 50% is held in more defensive fixed income bonds and gilts, 50% in global equities. For clients who generally score low on risk tests and have a limited appetite for the short-term fluctuations in equity markets. Expected growth rate is 5% per annum, net of fees and inflation.

■ Fixed Income   ▨ Equity

Figure 12 *Cautious sector weighting*

Balanced

Of this portfolio, 30% is held in more defensive fixed income bonds and gilts, 70% in global equities. For clients who generally score around the centre on risk tests, who have a limited appetite for the short-term fluctuations in daily equity prices but accept that they need to include a higher proportion of equity holdings to give them the potential for a better return over the longer term. Expected growth rate is 6% per annum, net of fees and inflation.

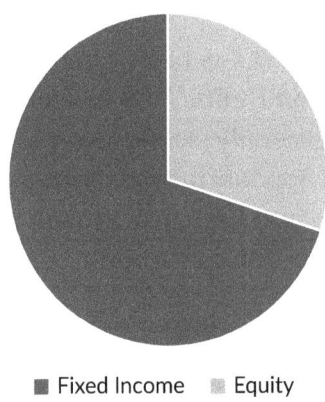

■ Fixed Income　▨ Equity

Figure 13 *Balanced sector weighting*

Adventurous

In this portfolio, 10% is held in more defensive fixed income bonds and gilts, 90% in global equities. For clients who generally score higher on risk tests and have a greater appetite for the movement in equity prices. Adventurous clients understand their capital values will move around far more than a balanced or cautious investor and the reward for accepting higher levels of volatility is the potential for returns to be higher. Expected growth rate is 7% per annum, net of fees and inflation.

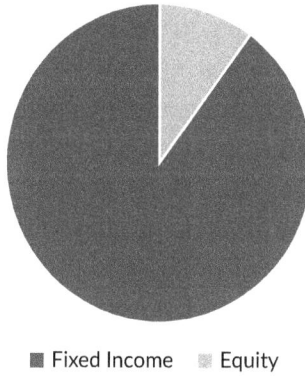

■ Fixed Income   Equity

Figure 14 *Adventurous sector weighting*

For anyone who thinks that 5% or 6% or even the 7% net annualised returns sound like low numbers then remember that some of the world's most successful investors are more than happy to pick up returns at that level, net of fees and inflation. It's not a glamorous return and it pales by comparison with the promises of 20% returns from the active advisers with their actively managed funds (NB these are usually gross returns; the net return will be lower) but the evidence I have found supports our strategy.

Another way to look at risk is to consider how a well-diversified portfolio of global equities compares to other asset classes. If you own 15,500 global equities in your pension or ISA, which you would with us, poor performers here and there should not have a significant effect; if you own 15 equities, 1 or 2 poor performers would likely have a major effect. If you decide to follow your stockbroker and invest in his new shiny company it might fail. What's the point in taking that risk when you can invest in a large number of small-cap companies (currently 4,533 are within our investment model, alongside 990 classed as value-cap, and 9,977 growth-cap or large-cap) all for *circa* 0.28% per year? Yes, here and there a few may fall over, but with exposure to that many you would have a very high level of diversification, and history has shown us you will receive the market return. When looking back five decades, that has been *circa* 14.7% annualised on the small-cap element. Here's how I explain risk.

Keep calm and think of the tuna

In the year I was born, 1972, the FTSE 100 in its old guise closed at just over 200 points. At the time of writing, it is floating at around 6,000 points, having dropped from its highest level, 7,847, in the first quarter of 2018. In the forty-nine years that I have been alive we have suffered some of the worst stock market declines in history.

I would be lying if I said it didn't bother me when I see the drops. It does. I can only tell you what I tell clients to do to. Put more in. Your head will be telling you not to do that. At that point you may even suggest my advice is bordering on the ridiculous. But putting more in during a dip is a good way to boost the whole pot and I'll do it every day of the week and twice on Sundays.

Not always, but typically, companies offering investments have made people think of these parameters when judging investment risk:

Table 12 *Typical risk categories*

Risk category	Asset type
1. Low risk	• Cash deposits
2. Medium risk	• Fixed income securities (gilts/bonds)
3. Higher risk	• Equities (stocks and shares)

This is misleading and a very poor guide. The following image backs up the grading we have shown above and is a real example from one pension providers key facts brochure. I don't think it could be any more unhelpful.

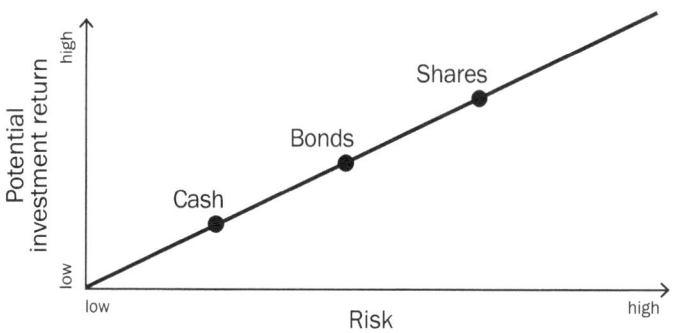

Figure 15 *Typical risk chart*

The company in question may well have the vertical axis showing an accurate reflection in terms of expected returns – as our data show, but the horizontal axis is misleading to say the least. Instead, what should be shared is something along the lines of what Andy Hart (Humans Under Management Ltd), coined his 'informed risk' chart. This was the blueprint for my extended version in Table 13, which is following a similar ethos. Investing into highly diversified equity and property funds (1–4) in my opinion, exposes you to very limited risk, in that the only dynamic you're likely to see is short-term price gyration. If you or your adviser deploy a mixed equity and fixed income fund (5) the same short-term exposure to price gyration will exist, just as it would had you opted for a full-blooded equity set up (although to a lesser extent, due to the fixed income element not moving around as much). However, do please remember that the evidence shows very clearly that adding in the fixed income element will likely also reduce your overall returns over time. Leaving your cash at the bank or building society, or investing it solely into fixed income investments (6–7), will see your capital attacked by inflation and its real value will diminish (as demonstrated earlier using the 1st class stamp). And risk is most certainly present in its highest form if you run with a limited equity model, or by sending your ISA or pension into a one sector fund, or if you follow what your sister's husband's uncle's boss, who runs his own haulage business told you to do (8–10). There's an old saying: if you need an

Table 13 Risk category per asset type and impact

Risk category	Asset type
1	• UK Large-Cap Equity Fund • Global Large-Cap Equity Fund • European Large-Cap Equity Fund
2	• UK Property Fund • Global Property Fund • European Property Fund
3	• UK Small-Cap and Value-Cap Equity Funds • Global Small-Cap and Value-Cap Equity Funds • European Small-Cap and Value-Cap Equity Funds
4	• Emerging World Large-Cap Equity Fund • Emerging World Small-Cap Equity Fund • Emerging World Value-Cap Equity Fund
5	• UK Equity/Fixed Income Fund • Global Equity/Fixed Income Fund • Emerging World Equity/Fixed Income Fund
6	• UK Gov./Corporate Bond Fund • Global Gov./Corporate Bond Fund • Emerging Gov./Corporate Bond Fund
7	• Cash at Bank • Building Society Deposits • National Savings/Premium Bonds
8	• Geographic or Sector Specific Equity Funds • Geographic or Sector Specific Fixed Income Funds • Global Commodity Fund
9	• Single Large-Cap Equity Stock • Single Fixed Income Bond • Single Global Commodity
10	• Single Small-Cap Equity Stock • Single Value-Cap Equity Stock • Current Top Tips

Which could be distilled down and summarised at a high level.

Risk category	Asset type
1. Low risk	• Highly Diversified Equity or Property Funds
2. Medium risk	• Highly Diversified Equity/Fixed Income Funds
3. Higher risk	• Cash Deposits, Fixed Income, Single Region/Sector/Company Equity

operation on your hip, don't ask the gardener to do it. Unfortunately, people out there are taking investment advice from people with Flymos every day of the week.

Instead, this is what should be shared.

The other suggestion I have is to buy in with regular amounts each month, quarter or whenever you can. That way you will buy stock as prices fluctuate and thus will sometimes be buying it cheap. Which is always good. Stock up when the tuna's on sale.

We educate our clients against selling out when the market tanks and, because they trust us, they don't make that mistake. They buy more, if they can. Everything in the investing conversation comes back to your number: the amount of money you'll need in order to live comfortably for over thirty years without the fear of running out of money, or dying with too much. And if you have a plan, we will have factored in the regular drops in any event. Your plan will be safe and robust if you don't give up on the strategy. It will work; even if you have to copy Peter, work a bit longer and retire in stages, because you didn't think about your retirement until your 40s.

Here is an exercise to help you find out the key detail we need to run an analysis on current arrangements. We do this at no cost with our Investment XRAY Service. When filling in the table, you need to decide on your number. This is the amount of annual income you would like to retire on. You also need to decide at what rate you would like this to grow throughout retirement.

Record here what funds you have in your various investment accounts, pensions, ISAs or other holdings. Jot down the name of the fund, the initial and ongoing costs and the amount of money you have invested. See if you can also find out if the fund is actively or passively managed, and then note the split of equity and fixed income. Your provider or adviser should be able to confirm this information without too much fuss. If it starts to feel like a problem, then… it's a problem.

Table 14 *Fund review matrix*

	Name	Initial fee (£ or %)	Annual fee (£ or %)	£ value	Fund strategy	Equity %	Bond %
Adviser							
Product/platform 1							
Fund 1							
Fund 2							
Fund 3							
Fund 4							
Fund 5							
Fund 6							
Fund 7							
Fund 8							
…							

That should set the scene and help you prepare a simple table showing the current important dynamics within your portfolio. You can download a more detailed XRAY template at www.martinwilcocks. co.uk/xray that also has an inflation adjustable investment return and capital depreciation calculator.

12

A for Allowances and Tax Planning

The allowance and tax planning session we run is not, never has been, and never will be, about tax avoidance. Tax avoidance schemes are toxic and are guaranteed to fall apart. Rather, our goal is to explore which of the many standard annual allowances (which are there for us all to use) our clients haven't used, or don't realise they're eligible for.

I'm all for finding ways that make best use of our annual allowances within the legal boundaries we have in place. Trying to drive around the boundaries with expensive schemes is often more risk and trouble than it's worth. Just take a look online at the numbers of well-known celebrities and sports stars who get caught up.

To help clients reduce their business and personal taxes and maximise the return on their investments, we look at straightforward options such as:

- Capital Gains Tax annual exemption
- Inheritance Tax annual gift exemption
- ISA allowance
- Pensions
- Higher tax rate
- Dividend allowance

Capital Gains Tax annual exemption

For 2020–21 this exemption for all individuals was set at £12,300. I might advise clients to sell down investments that have gained, to use their allowances, or consider a transfer of assets between spouses so that both can benefit from the annual exemption.

Inheritance Tax annual gift exemption

Often clients don't take full advantage of the annual gift exemption, which has remained at £3,000 for several years. If it's not been claimed from the previous year, then £6,000 can be claimed in the current year. There are also exemptions for other small gifts, and wedding gifts for children and grandchildren, and gifts to charitable and political organisations, can help bring down IHT on an estate.

Further gifts can be made from excess surplus income, that is not needed. If a parent or grandparent has, by way on an example, £12,000 per year surplus from their total income, this can be gifted and is immediately classed as being outside of one's estate. If the £12,000 annual surplus builds up over twenty years to £240,000, whilst it remains inside the estate, perhaps losing value sat at the building society, it could eventually be liable to IHT with potentially 40% (£96,000) passing to HMRC. Rather than hand it over to the government, could it not have been used inside the family unit instead? If you have grand-children, you could, using this example, reduce your estate, mitigate IHT and watch the children flourish at school, or university, all at the same time. Just a thought.

ISA allowance

Up to £20,000 can be invested in an ISA every year completely free of capital gains tax and income tax. You can also invest for your children with an additional junior ISA limit of £9,000 for under 18's.

Pensions

They remain one of the most tax-efficient and flexible ways to save for retirement. The annual allowance (AA; maximum we can put in that qualifies for tax relief) is £40,000. At present, for those with an income above £150,000, there is a reduction in that annual allowance and, as such, the available tax relief is reduced. It appears to the be the case that HMRC is watching carefully at how much tax relief it is giving away, or rather, passing back.

You may carry forward any AA not used in the previous three years. The current tax year's AA must be used in full first. Tax relief is granted in full for the year the contribution is made. Those with no contributions in the three years to 6 April 2020 could carry forward up to £120,000, and would still have an AA of up to £40,000 for 2020–21.

Higher tax rate

Where clients have an income over £100,000, their higher tax rate (up to a maximum of 60%) could be reduced if they make pension contributions, Gift Aid payments, and defer income such as dividends.

Dividend allowance

Clients don't have to pay tax on the first £2,000 of their dividend income, no matter what non-dividend income they have. And if other members of the family also work in the business, which can be common, they too can be appointed, perhaps as a company director, and have a £2,000 personal allowance. The business can then also make pension contributions for its directors, on which it receives corporation tax relief.

That's the top and bottom of my tax planning. There's nothing exciting about it, but millions of people every year fail to use these standard allowances and my goal is to encourage our clients to take advantage of them.

Schemes to view with caution

There are other allowances that I steer away from. The Enterprise Investment Scheme (EIS) and Seed Enterprise Investment Scheme (SEIS) give tax breaks for investing in newer companies and start-ups. When they work, they can have a huge positive impact on our economy in many ways, including creating thousands of jobs. These schemes are not aggressive, in the sense tax avoidance schemes are, but they are not for me. I worry about the clients who will blame me and tell everyone they know that I'm an idiot when the EIS they invest in falls apart: many do. I've said many times in this book that I believe in investing in the whole market, not gambling on individual companies. With income tax relief on the way in, and with a tax-efficient investment, EIS/SEIS might sound great, but what if the company fails? So, if it's an EIS you want I'm not the adviser for you. Anyway, for what it's worth, I'll describe these schemes.

Enterprise Investment Scheme (EIS)

EIS is a higher-risk, tax-efficient investment. Investments generate a 30% income tax credit to offset against income tax liabilities in the year the investment is made (or they can be carried back into the previous tax year). You may invest up to £1,000,000 a year in an EIS and all gains will be free from capital gains tax after three years.

Seed EIS (SEIS)

For those with a very high tolerance for risk, Seed EIS offers 50% income tax credit for investments in very small businesses within the UK, plus allows up to 14% capital gains tax relief on the way in. You may invest up to £100,000 a year in a Seed EIS and all gains will be free from capital gains tax after three years.

Venture Capital Trust (VCT)

VCT is a highly tax-efficient investment scheme designed to provide private equity capital for small, expanding companies, and income and/or capital gains for investors. You may invest up to £200,000 a year in a VCT.

These three options are all clean, in my opinion; but all go against the investment approach I've outlined in this book. While some tax planners will make a song and dance around how they must dive down deep into your tax matters our tax planning session is always kept simple. Make a note in Table 15 of what you have used against these basic tax allowances in the last three years and have a think about what you could have done differently. There may be an opportunity to explore mopping up unused allowances in certain cases and any good adviser should be looking at that.

Table 15 Pension allowances used

	2020	2019	2018
Pension AA used			
ISA allowances used			
CGT allowance used			

For those of you wishing to explore the tax incentives of the more esoteric types of investment, EIS, SEIS and VCT, there are many companies available to help you. One specialist tax consultancy is Moneyspider Consultancy (www.moneyltd.co.uk), who can offer a dedicated tax mitigation service. These alternative investments are not wrong; as I said, they are just not for us.

13

R for Risk Management

Back in April 2018 Ernst & Young reported that SwissRe had estimated that people in the UK are buying £2.4 trillion less insurance cover than we need to ensure that our families and dependants can maintain their standard of living if we should die, or become seriously ill, tomorrow.[17] There may be a more recent figure but it doesn't matter; the last time I looked, in my last year at Barclays, the 'protection gap' was about the same. As a result of this shortfall both private individuals and business owners are carrying huge risks, which could create enormous pain and suffering should premature death or illness occur.

Plugging the gap

In this area of our planning, we get to the heart of the risks that exist in our client's business and plug the gaps. At the same time, we make sure that the family is considered in the decision making and will be properly looked after if a catastrophe does happen.

For the family, we look back at the crucial target level of post-retirement income and work out how much money we would need to drop into 'the bank account' today, if death or illness occurred, to provide that target income for your spouse and any children. By simply looking back at the lifestyle financial plan and pension goal, we can calculate the shortfall as of today, and provide for the family should premature death or illness occur between now and retirement.

This I would suggest is a better way of deciding how much life and serious illness cover you might need than plucking numbers from thin air, perhaps using a comparison website or a high street provider to explore what should be a very important decision. A comparison site cannot show any interest in your hopes, dreams and aspirations. It can only churn out a number. How many breadwinners simply say 'I need £200,000 of life cover and I'll get that sorted on one of those comparison sites and crack on', only for their family to find out after their premature death that ten times that might be needed to get the children through to age 21?

The financial plan needs a backstop that is typically an insurance policy, or a series of policies, to cover catastrophe scenarios that would impact on the family or your business, such as critical illness, serious injury or sudden premature death.

It is essential that is it spoken about, if you don't want to leave your loved ones high and dry should the worst happen. It's no different to locking a large lump sum away in a safe, just in case. This is risk management.

How much cover is enough?

Have a think about the amount of cover you might need, using Table 16.

Table 16 Risk management planner

Outstanding mortgage =

Other debts =

Current annual income × 10 =

Current annual income × number of years before youngest child reaches 21 =

There is no hard and fast rule to working out the amount of life and illness cover you might need and there are no wrong or right answers. I have shown that a huge gap exists and it is clear that people aren't insuring themselves properly, regardless of whether you agree with the multiples I have suggested. My aim in this instance is to get you thinking about it realistically.

A decent adviser will explore these dynamics with you. As a rough guide, if you worked off something like what I've suggested above you would be within a golf shot of what your family would need. In my view they would need to be debt-free, with a substantial lump sum right now (I suggest ten times what you're earning, after taxes as a starting point for planning): if invested properly that should protect your lifestyle.

I also believe if your youngest child is aged 11, like my son Oscar, you probably need another ten years' income on top, to get them to a non-dependent age (say, 21). Some parents with 21-year-old children may be shouting that they still need support once they're 'independent'. Like I said, there is no right or wrong answer.

Other aspects of family life might dictate a longer-term need, even one that may never expire. A whole-of-life requirement is common, for example, if you have a disabled child, an IHT liability or are responsible financially for other family members and couldn't put a time limit on when your need for cover might diminish. You might want to distinguish needs with a time limit (term) from whole-of-life needs. Note your numbers from Table 16 and do this quick test to summarise where a conversation with your financial planner could start:

Table 17 *Family cover planner*

| Fixed term | Y/N | Amount: £ |
| Whole of life | Y/N | Amount: £ |

Legal & General's *State of the Nation's SMEs Report* reports that, of the 5.5 million small and medium-sized enterprises (private sector businesses) in the UK, a staggering 48% had made no protection provision.[18]

Lack of protection for businesses

Lack of protection leads to a great many worrying problems for the business owner:

1. With no shareholder protection, there could be insufficient funds to buy back the shares if a shareholder died or became seriously ill.

2. If no key person profit protection is in place, there is no safety net to provide a vital injection of capital into the business if a key driver of the business profit falls ill or dies.

3. Any bank borrowings or loan accounts might need to be repaid if an owner, shareholder, or even a director who the bank considers to be important, dies suddenly or cannot run the business due to critical illness.

My approach is a robust company will, alongside a properly thought-out shareholding and profit protection plan. But, as the numbers show, almost half of our businesses don't bother, leaving everything they are building at risk of collapse should something go wrong. Not having a viable contingency plan is like building your business on quicksand.

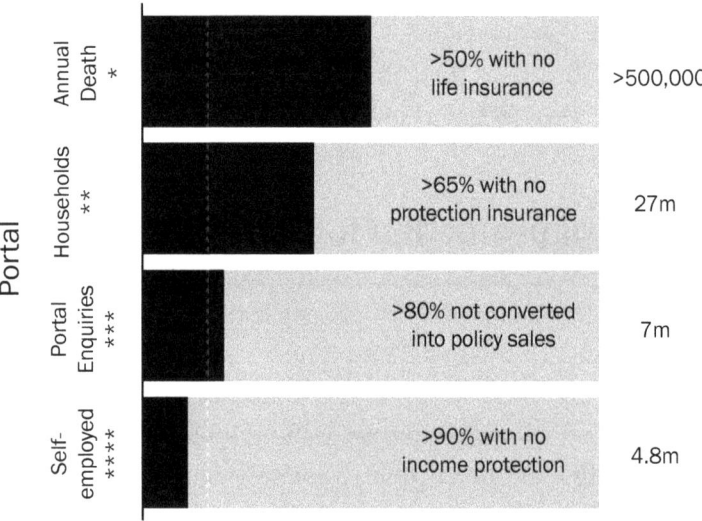

Figure 16 The £2.4 trillion gap in protection.

Source: *ONS, YouGov, Myles Rx; ** ABI, Myles Rx; ***Steve Marshal, Reassured; *** ONS, Swiss Re

Table 18 Business Protection Planner

Gross profit x 5 (Company valuation) =

Ownership*

Shareholder 1	shareholding %	=
Shareholder 2	shareholding %	=
Shareholder 3	shareholding %	=
Shareholder 4	shareholding %	=

*All shareholders should have life assurance for the equivalent value of their equity, written in trust to the other shareholders (such that they would have the monetary value of a deceased, or seriously ill shareholders equity, to buy the shares back from the ill owner or his/her surviving spouse, to maintain the company's stability). At the same time a surviving spouse will often want the capital value of his or her deceased partner,s equity, rather than a stake and position in the company.

Profits*

Profit Contributor Key Person 1	=
Profit Contributor Key Person 2	=
Profit Contributor Key Person 3	=
Profit Contributor Key Person 3	=

*If one or more members of the team, and not necessarily the owners, are pivotal to the firms profits then it can be sensible for the company to insure itself against any loss of profit that results from such a person not being able to work or contribute, again due to death or illness. As a guide, the company may consider protecting itself for five years whilst a replacement key person is identified, brought into the company and bedded in. There is no right or wrong answer and all situations are different.

Debts*

Debts*	=
Directors Loans	=
Bank Loans	=
Overdrafts	=
Asset Finance	=

*If a shareholder, or key person, again vital to the company's success, dies or becomes ill, it may be sensible to pay off any debts to alleviate financial pressure as the business adjusts. The bank may also be nervous at the loss of such an individual and insist that borrowings are repaid. If a director is owed money, in his or her director's loan account, and passes away, a similar issue as per the overall ownership can be a problem. A seriously ill director with a positive director's loan account is likely to want that money back. As would the surviving spouse if the individual in question was to pass away.

14

E for Estate Planning

The risk management session paves the way to address what is the final taboo for most people: what happens when they die. As a nation we appear to be gripped by an estate planning apathy, an almost out-and-out failure to look ahead. Newspapers regularly report that around half of UK adults have failed to make a basic will. Inheritance tax receipts at HMRC have been rising year on year ever since IHT took over from capital transfer tax in the 1970s. In the last two decades, HMRC has collected an annual IHT bumper prize bounty of between £2 billion and £5 billion. The payment of this voluntary tax demonstrates a complete lack of planning.

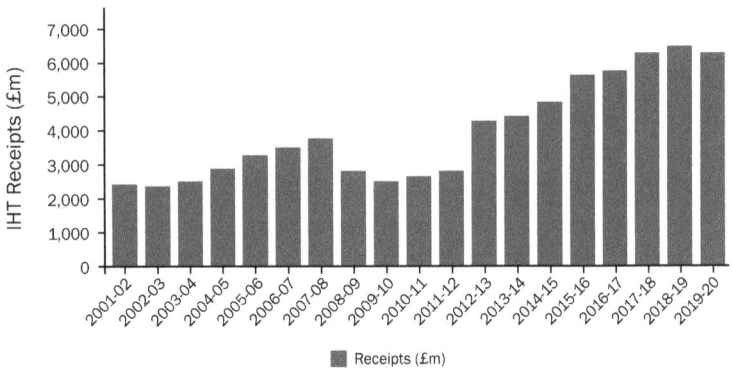

Figure 17 IHT receipts, 2001–20. Source: HMRC

Gloomy as it might sound, we must all think about the consequences of death. Most people simply fail to ensure that their estates pass to their loved ones safely and tax-efficiently. There are many problems within the estate planning space which may indicate why so many people close their eyes and hope for the best.

Ten steps to 'kick-start estate planning'

1. **Is there a will in place (or would the laws of intestacy kick in)?**

   With no will, the law of intestacy will see the government control the distribution of estate assets. If you are married or in a civil partnership and have no children, all of your estate will go to your spouse or civil partner. If you do have children, the first £270,000 will go to your spouse or civil partner, along with any personal possessions. Anything over £270,000 will then be divided, with your spouse or civil partner receiving 50% and the children entitled to divide the other 50% between them. This may not always be a bad plan, but the main point is that Intestacy laws can change, and whatever the case may be, without a will, control of the estate is not in your camp.

2. **If your children are minors, who would look after them if you died?**

It is almost unbearable to think about what happens where both parents die. It is certainly not what you and your spouse want to think about when you get a rare weekend away. But I do advise thinking about it at some point.

Unless guardians have been appointed, social services would decide on your children's future, adding further distress at a critical time in their lives. Your decision needs to be discussed with siblings, or other appropriate members of your family, and documented properly. Do what I call a 'reverse option deal' over dinner and a bottle of wine with your intended guardians. Just do it.

3. **Have you arranged lasting powers of attorney?**

Every year, thousands of people attend the Court of Protection to gain 'deputyship'. This will let them handle the financial and property affairs, and the health and wellbeing, of loved ones who have fallen ill or been in an accident and are no longer competent to look after their own affairs. It's not a fast-track process (it can take six to nine months) and it generally involves paying a solicitor to sort it all out, creating extra anxiety at an already stressful time. Being married does not automatically entitle a spouse to handle your affairs. Deputyship will have to be awarded by the Court of Protection if robust powers of attorney have not already been put in place.

4. **What should happen if one spouse passes?**

Many problems can develop if an estate is simply passed between spouses on first death. Tax implications can arise and at worst a family's entire estate can ultimately pass to a different bloodline. What happens if I die, my wife later remarries, and then dies herself? With no proper will in place our estate could pass sideways to someone else. The courts are full of contested 'second marriage' probate cases every week. Decide what you want to happen and document your wishes clearly.

5. **Would the estate pass directly to beneficiaries on the second spouse passing?**

This could be a dangerous problem for a large estate. If your children will inherit a nominal amount there is not much risk to them, but what if they are still young and inherit a large amount?

What if they are targeted by unscrupulous people? What if they get into trouble?

No one likes to think of these problems but I'm afraid they arise quite often. How would you feel about this? Would it be better to set up a protective structure that ring-fences the estate, but allows your children (or other dependants) controlled access to it?

6. Is there an inheritance tax problem?

Since 2000 HMRC has collected between £2 billion and £5.5 billion every year in this tax.[19] If the estate is above the nil rate band (currently £325,000 for a single person and £650,000 for a married couple), 40% of the excess will pass to HMRC, which could have been enjoyed by or used to educate children or grandchildren. It's not difficult to mitigate IHT, by using the annual allowances in a spending and gifting programme rather than leaving the estate to build up. IHT avoidance schemes exist, but can be expensive to set up and/or complex to run. I don't advise them. If it goes wrong you'll incur high legal costs, a large fine and then all the tax you were trying to avoid paying – or your family will, if this comes to light after you die.

7. Have you considered later-life care?

The social care system in the UK is at breaking point, predominantly due to massive population growth since the end of the Second World War. In fact, the UK population has more than doubled from around 30 million to nearly 70 million in those seventy years, and many of us are living longer than our parents' generation did. The *Daily Mail* has said that up to 20,000 people have to sell their homes every year to fund basic care in old age.[20] That's fifty-five properties every day that would otherwise have passed to beneficiaries. Before the elders lose their homes, they first must hand over all their savings. They are left with nothing to pass on to their children. We really should be planning for our later years alongside that dream retirement. It's older age rather than old age that needs to be factored into the plan: I'll say from age 85 to make the point. Like our friend Peter, maybe we will need to stage our retirement or do some consultancy work.

8. Have you appointed executors and trustees?

If you don't appoint someone to administer your estate after your death the government will take care of it; and we know that probably won't work out well. The executor's job is to carry out the estate instructions. At least one highly trusted family member or close friend (anyone that you consider suitable and of sound mind) should be appointed, along with a reputable external professional who should be appointed to act as a sounding board.

If you have set up a trust, the trustees could act on a 'letter of wishes' (LOW). These letters are a guide to what should happen, for example with payments to children. If you decide to 'ring-fence' your estate, your family or other legatees do not own it, the trust does, and that can save a lot of problems. The trustee(s) can be guided (though a LOW is not binding on them) to ensure that any trusts do their job and protect the family unit. Drafting the trust deed (or whatever documentation you use) needs to be done carefully to ensure the trust operates the way you want it to.

9. **Are there any specific gifts or legacies?**

    You might wish to leave specific gifts to family members or friends; perhaps financial or personal items like jewellery or cars. Are they to be of equal importance, and should anyone be specifically excluded from the list? It is sensible to consider all matters, including previous relationships, and refer to these in the will so that a contentious probate is avoided.

10. **Do you have any funeral wishes?**

    For many people, the decision on burial or cremation is the main element of a will. You will now have realised that it's the least important point in many ways, but nonetheless your wishes are still worth noting, to make decisions easier for your loved ones. Do you want to leave specific instructions about speakers, readings, music and so on?

Here Is An Exercise: Think Of Your Time On This Planet Coming To An End In An Oscar-Winning Theatrical Filmset Farewell, Then Fill In The Chart.

- F is for funeral. Is it a burial or cremation, and what should they all sing?
- I is for intestacy. Did you make a will or did the government call the shots?
- L is for legacies. Who got what, when and in what proportions?
- M is for minors. Did you appoint guardians or leave it up to social services?
- S is for spouse. Did everything simply pass or did you protect the bloodline?
- E is for excluded. Who could contest your will, why would they, and how?
- T is for tax. How much will the chancellor and his civil servants get to spend?

F	
I	
L	
M	
S	
E	
T	

Summary

Quite often during estate planning, it transpires that complex wills are required: perhaps to set up post-death trusts to handle the ring-fencing we discussed above, or to hold agricultural or business assets because by doing so we can mitigate and reduce IHT.

Integrated family trusts can also be set up during your lifetime, predominantly to capture 'today's wealth' and, where possible, control 'future wealth', tax-efficiencies and capital distribution for family members. Trusts can protect spouses and children, and could be arranged to split the estate for effective and tax-efficient distribution after you die, or to provide for various situations during the rest of your life.

Other trusts can be set up, for example, to house employer's death-in-service payments, to further reduce the potential for inheritance tax to be levied against the estate.

An estate or, rather, we as individuals should also be supported via lasting powers of attorney. Health affairs should be under one power and property and financial matters under another. Additionally, a family investment company could provide further layers of financial and investment planning, both to maximise the estate's value and to manage its tax position, and this could be deployed when estates reach a certain size, which is always subjective of course. The overriding point being, in my opinion, the estate would typically be in touching distance of a seven figure sum, as a minimum, and more often than not, a lot more. There is no point paying 45% income tax on investments if a company can make the same investments and pay 19% corporation tax. (NB It costs something to set up and run a company, so this approach is not cost-effective for everybody.) This is not tax evasion, it is legal, legitimate tax mitigation based financial planning.

This stage of the CLEARER™ process helps clients to gain a much broader perspective on why they need a solid, dependable and deliverable plan that will cater for their needs and protect their loved ones. For many people, it's the first time that they begin to fully understand not only the importance of estate planning, but also that there are numerous options that can be tailored to their unique circumstances.

15

R for Review

People are constantly busy. It's little wonder, there- fore, that they don't have time to work out the amount of money they'll need to finance their ideal lifestyle once retired. The problems such busy people face extend way past knowing the magic number and might include:

- How suitable their investments and pensions are

- Whether they have used their various tax allowances effectively

- If they have left their family and fellow business owners and shareholders protected if disaster strikes

- If they have made a succession plan to pass on their wealth to children and other beneficiaries safely and tax-efficiently

The CLEARER™ wealth management process is built specifically with the busy client in mind. Our final Review stage regularly takes the temperature of each client's plan at agreed times, to check that it's all still running as intended.

This is more than just checking the plan. It's an opportunity to adapt it to take account of changing circumstances; and to help the relationship between adviser and client develop. It's an important and rewarding element of what we do because it often involves food and wine and as we plan, the trust we build grows stronger.

Clients may be a number somewhere else, but to me the client families I currently look after are, and always will be, an extension of my own family, and will benefit from the highest levels of service and protection. And the service will always seek to ensure they secure an income they can't outlive and a legacy to their children… or other beneficiaries.

Value-added scorecard

In my old corporate roles, a review was a quick pit stop where you'd ask about the family etc. All nice, but perhaps lacking substance. So, along with engaging a great coach (Brett Davidson), we developed a scorecard to work out the value we add for our clients each year, which was perhaps passing under the radar. This live example scorecard below is a small part of what we created with Brett's help and shows how we record, track and value our input.

Table 19 Value-added spreadsheet

	Value Added	Value
Value		
Investment		
Costs Saved	£2,660	£380k in previous advisers funds - costs reduced from 1% to 0.3% - saving £2660 pa
Total:	£2,660	
Tax		
Pension tax savings	£8,000	Gross pension contribution of £40K using unused tax relief from 2016-2019
CGT tax savings	£3,800	Part of annual CGT allowance utilised by disinvesting non-ISA fund
Income tax savings		
NI Savings		
Total:	£11,800	
Education/Entertainment		
Entertainment	£200	Post-review private lunch to catch up properly
Seminars		
Blogs	£0	Shared 2 relevant blogs on passive beating active (investment management)
Total:	£200	

Continued

Table 19 Value-added spreadsheet ctd.

	Value Added	Value
Estate Planning		
Wills Established	£475	Wrote 2 wills at no cost in respect of ongoing relationship
Trusts established	£475	Included lasting powers of attorney, again in respect of ongoing relationship
IHT Saved		
Total:	£950	
Problems Avoided		
Recommendations to NOT do something	£26,800	Not buying the 6 bed development - SDLT & legal bill alone was £7,312
Strategies or Structures established that avoid problems in future		
Total:	£26,800	
Other Professionals		
Referrals to other professionals	£750	2 hours of time with your new accountant
Tax saved as a result		Yet to materialise but should prove successful
Costs avoided as a result		
Any benefits from advice given - pension freedom	£1,500	Advice to brother and wife
Investment opportunities		
Total:	£2,250	
Administration Hassle		
Complaint with Barclays	£600	Bank refunded this to you
Dealing with Barclays	£750	2 hours of time
Total:	£1,350	
Miscallaneous		
Cost of Loan (3%)	£1,500	Specified loan be paid off saving interest
Total:	£1,500	

Continued

Table 19 Value-added spreadsheet ctd.

	Value Added	Value
Portfolio Total	£1,285,000	
Total:	£47,510	Saved / added value
Value Add (%)	3.70%	
Fee	£12,850	

Conclusion

Planning your retirement isn't about making painful decisions; it's about avoiding painful consequences. Proper financial planning can have a massive impact not just on your life, but also on those of your children and their children. Intergenerational wealth planning focuses on family, not just on money.

My advice, as I've advocated throughout this book, is don't procrastinate any longer. Work out the income necessary for you to achieve that lifestyle you crave and the magic number that will allow you to maintain that throughout retirement, without either running out of money or perhaps, worst of all, dying with too much having not enjoyed it while you still had the chance.

Question your adviser and find out whether the investments you hold are on or off track. Are you making full use of your corporation tax, income tax and capital gains tax allowances effectively, every year? Have you protected your business or your family in the event of death or illness? The last thing you want is to leave your estate in chaos, so please make your will. Plan your legacy so that beneficiaries, and not HMRC, gain from all your hard work.

Perhaps after reading this book, you may feel more confident in having a conversation with your current financial adviser about whether your plan is evidence-based or fully maximises your tax allowances. Ask them about the risks and whether there's anything lurking under the surface that could damage your family's prospects should something untoward happen to you. Their reaction will probably tell you more than their actual response and you'll know whether you're paying too much for advice from an adviser more interested in the money than they are in you.

To help you take your first steps, you can download my free XLS template, which helps you gather your current pension and investments information, by using this: www.martinwilcocks.co.uk/xray.

You can also watch my free video series here: www.martinwilcocks.co.uk/videos.

After reading this book, you should feel more confident about how to navigate forwards. I will leave you with a few final thoughts, which do not constitute investment advice, rather they form my general and personal opinions.

If your capital is invested into debt; fixed-income securities, it would be remiss of me not to point out the big (I say big, but let me be clear, they are potentially huge) problems that I think you will have going forward, so please allow me to do that in an attempt to help you get through your retirement years, whilst maintaining your ideal standard of living, and never run out of money. I want to bring something very important back to the centre of your attention, something that we have touched on and I hope illustrates just how crucial it is that you take proper financial advice. The sooner you do, the better the chances of securing an uncompromised retirement.

Back in 1990, a first-class stamp was 22p. At the time of writing the closing chapters in this book, the same first-class stamp was 76p. It is now over three times more expensive than it was back then to put a letter in the post. I expect the same three-fold rise to happen over the next thirty years, which will uplift the cost of sending your first-class letter to around £2.50. Fixed-income returns, when adjusted against inflation, will not see your capital rise sufficiently to cover the cost of posting a letter. You will have to deliver your own post on foot, or a bicycle, firstly because the stamp will feel expensive against your income and secondly because you will not be in a position to cover the cost of whatever transportation is equal to a car today.

Be equally aware if you are invested in a mixed-asset fund (eg 20–60% or 40–85%), which is, broadly speaking, in my opinion, just a proportionate notch up from the fixed income set-up. Then we have the cash sat at the bank (we all know what that delivers). Wealth eroding inflation will continue to attack returns from cash deposits and fixed income.

The 'industry' says something that was probably concocted in the national insurer's institute boardroom, with a number cruncher and compliance manager: 'As they get older, put them all into fixed income. Decrease their exposure to equity and increase their fixed income and keep doing it as they get older. They won't see the money shift around in value that much so won't start to panic. That way we will keep everyone calm and stop millions of retired people calling their pension or insurance companies every minute of the day, in tears, screaming that they are losing money.'

I paint an exaggerated scene, but it's an assimilation of the situation as I see it, and I share my take on it to deliver the detail, that you need to be aware of. The other point to note about this silly 'lifestyling' malarkey, is that it's been going on for years, and as far back as when people retired at 65 and passed at 70 (which wasn't that long ago).

Unfortunately, notwithstanding various attempts by the government, during my time at least, to both promote the use of and simplify pensions, they still can often be running this very outdated strategy. Pensions were designed years ago to help people get from retirement age to 'not very further forward' due to lower longevity, but retirement has evolved so much over the years and we can all now expect to last far longer. However, the 'pension product' in many cases hasn't adapted or moved on. It's a bit like the highway code. The analogy here for example is that the motorway speed limit of 70 mph was set many years ago based on vehicle braking distances. But my current car can brake from 70 mph to zero three times faster than my old Mark 1 Escort did, but the limit is still 70 mph. It's stuck, just like lifestyling.

Alas, thanks to medical advances, better diets, and us being generally more health-conscious, thankfully, we are all living approximately 10–15 years longer and getting to 90 is no longer unusual. Time magazine wrote about '2045 man'[21] in the recent past and some out there think that in the next couple of decades we will morph into semi-human, semi-cyborgs and old age will be a thing people look back on in time and scratch their heads saying, 'What on earth did they let people die for?'.

Yes, this is all very extreme, I grant you, and I am not so sure. What I am sure of is first, retirement planning has never been so important as it now is and, second, however old you are when the time finally comes, your fixed-income portfolio will have long been extinguished. It will not stand the test of time; of that I am certain.

And remember the passive vs active dynamic. The buy and hold strategy has been proven to beat the active – get in at the top and back out at the bottom/repeat, alternative, all week long, and twice on Sundays. Also remember fees, because just 1% in excess cost will see you pay away the same amount you invested, over a thirty-year time horizon. Thus, saving that 1%, and retaining it in your portfolio, will be equivalent to your initial investment stake, which you can use to go on lots of holidays, help your children and grandchildren out, and even make a difference within an organisation or charity whose work you admire, value and respect.

Equity market gyration is the price we must pay for an income we cannot outlive and to help us make those further investments into legacies that will live on, long after we pass. Without proper help from an adviser to stand alongside you, helping you to make the right choices and stopping you from serious irreparable financial self-harm when the inevitable cycles land, when markets and prices drop, you may take a few wrong turns that will cause you to run out of money. And it may well happen far quicker than you might think. Just look at the stamps.

I fear that without proper help and advice, you may be like a ship at sea with a broken compass, struggling to reach your desired retirement destination.

My CLEARER™ process can be followed by anyone. It doesn't need to be hard work but, like anything, the first step is always the biggest. If that's where you are now, then don't be afraid, take that step and ask those questions, because this is the beginning of your journey towards becoming bulletproof. You'll be glad that you did.

Alternatively, take advantage of an exclusive reader offer for a twenty-minute initial consultation in which myself or a team member can explore how they might be able to support you further. You can book your consultation directly using this link: https://meetings.hubspot.com/martin132.

I have created an online course that will take you through each step of my CLEARER™ model providing a blueprint and route to your success. It's packed with demonstrations, my level 2,3 and 4 videos, plus takeaways in each section to hold your hand and encourage fast implementation. In this Bulletproof™ course, my entire thirty years of experience is passed on in a highly visual, helpful, and constructive way and, providing each step is followed, I pledge there will be at least one golden nugget in each of my six CLEARER™ sections for everyone. In most cases, I estimate the tangible value to be highly significant and, in some cases, lifechanging. See how my Bulletproof™ online course can help steer your own financial future here: www.martinwilcocks.co.uk/bulletproofcourse.

References

1 Figure based on data from the Office for National Statistics, www.ons.gov.uk, accessed 12 August 2021.

2 Murray, N, *The Excellent Investment Advisor* (Southold, NY: Nick Murray Co. Inc., 1996).

3 Finch, D (2017), *Live long and prosper? Demographic trends and their implications for living standards* (Resolution Foundation, 2017), www.resolutionfoundation.org/publications/ live-long-and-prosper-demographic-trends-and- their-implications-for-living-standards, accessed 13 July 2021.

4 The Investment Association, *Investment management in the UK 2019–2020: The Investment Association annual survey* (September 2020), www.theia.org/sites/default/files/2020-

09/20200924-imsfullreport.pdf, accessed 12 August 2021.

5   Plagge, J-C et al., *The case for low-cost index-fund investing* (Vanguard, April 2021), www.vanguardinvestments.se/documents/institutional/low-cost-index-fund-investing-eu.pdf, accessed 17 August 2021.

6   Flood, C, 'Warren Buffett tells wife: go cheap and passive', *Financial Times* (7 March 2014), www.ft.com/content/0fdc605a-a53d-11e3-8988-00144feab7de

7   The Editorial Board, 'Jack Bogle" the selfless preacher of the passive revolution', *Financial Times* (18 January 2019), www.ft.com/content/7a2a0aa0-1a5b-11e9-9e64-d150b3105d21

8   World Federation of Exchanges database, *Listed domestic companies, total*, https://data.worldbank.org/indicator/CM.MKT.LDOM.NO, accessed 12 August 2021.

9   Financial Conduct Authority, *Our mission 2017: How we regulate financial services* (October 2016, updated July 2021), www.fca.org.uk/publication/corporate/our-mission-2017.pdf, accessed 20 April 2022.

10 Wilcocks, M, *Will small-cap and value-cap equities do in the next seven decades what they did in the last seven?* (Wilcocks & Wilcocks Wealth Management, 12 August 2021), https://martinwilcocks.co.uk/will-small-cap-and-value-cap-equities-do-in-the-next-seven-decades-

what-they-did-in-the-last-seven, accessed 17 August 2021.

11   Sommer, J, 'Mutual fund winners don't stay ahead for long', *The New York Times* (31 July 2020), www.nytimes.com/2020/07/31/business/mutual-fund-winners-stocks-bonds.html, accessed 12 August 2021.

12   Data provided by Dimensional Fund Advisors Ltd, used with permission.

13   Murray, N, *The Excellent Investment Advisor* (Southold, NY: Nick Murray Co. Inc., 1996).

14   Datablog, 'Stamp prices: how have they changed since 1980?', The Guardian (2016), www.theguardian.com/news/datablog/2012/mar/27/60p-price-stamp-royal-mail, accessed 20 April 2022.

15   Image based on information gained using the Bank of England's inflation calculator available at www.bankofengland.co.uk/monetary-policy/inflation/inflation-calculator, accessed 17 August 2021.

16   Financial Conduct Authority, *Review on disclosure of costs by asset managers* (February 2019), www.fca.org.uk/publications/multi-firm-reviews/review-disclosure-costs-asset-managers, accessed 20 April 2022.

17   Allison, C, *Why the UK protection insurance industry is missing out on opportunities* (Ernst & Young LLP, 12 April 2018), www.ey.com/en_gl/financial-services-emeia/why-the-uk-protection-insurance-industry-is-missing-out-on-opportunities, accessed 16 July 2021.

18 Legal & General, *Business protection: State of the nation's SMEs report. Fifth edition* (Legal & General, 2017), www.legalandgeneral.com/files/library/protection/sales-aid/w13220.pdf, accessed 16 July 2021.

19 UK Government, Inheritance Tax Statistics (last updated 29 July 2021), www.gov.uk/government/collections/inheritance-tax-statistics, accessed 17 August 2021.

20 Martin, D, 'Thousands more elderly forced to sell their homes as care home fees soar to £26,000', *The Daily Mail* (30 May 2011), www.dailymail.co.uk/news/article-1392251/Care-home-fees-soar-26-000-year--thousands-elderly-forced-sell-homes.html, accessed 12 August 2021.

21 Grossman, L, '2045: The Year Man Becomes Immortal', *TIME* (10 February 2011), https://ti.me/1fhZdiQ, accessed 26 May 2022

22 Murray, N, *The Excellent Investment Advisor* (Southold, NY: Nick Murray Co. Inc., 1996).

Acknowledgements

Back in 1989 Lois Hughes, my first manager at Barclays in Little Sutton, asked me, as she was sipping her super-strong black coffee, and whilst bouncing the day's bad cheques I had taken to her, 'Are you sure this is the right career for you, Martin?' Her challenge has always stayed with me like a calling, and I make sure every day that yes, I am still pursuing the right career.

Malcolm Doughty, a senior corporate manager, introduced me to how the bank did its business whilst I was at Barclays' Liverpool Victoria Street Branch in the early 1990s at Ye Hole in Ye Wall each lunchtime, over four pints, a ham bap and a plate of chips. His wise counsel continued during our time at Barclays in Chester, at The Marlborough Arms.

Nigel Gallagher and Steve Tennant prised me from the clutches of the retail bank in 1998 and finally persuaded me to 'give financial planning a try' after a number of their predecessors had not quite convinced me, and that shifted the course of my career. I must also thank my family and friends for giving me the courage, once I was on my new path, to go off-piste and set up my own business.

Everything we have invested in to help our business grow adds value in our clients' lives. I'd like to mention especially:

- Paul Armson and his private one-to-one coaching and Financial Planning training, which helped Wilcocks & Wilcocks develop the detailed one-to-one coaching that is our trademark, helping us move past selling products and into developing our CLEARER™ model, which makes a difference in our clients' lives – our investment has been repaid at least 100-fold and has added immense value for clients

- Brett Davidson and his FP Advance Course was of huge value to us and it continues to add further value in our clients' lives

- David Swanwick, Harry Walker and Tom Fellowes who all took a trip 'up north' to see two brothers in their Liverpool office all those years ago, and since then everyone else with whom we continue to engage at Dimensional Fund

Advisors, including Elliott Poole and Weston Wellington (who to this day still has the funniest and most engaging presentation on investing I've ever seen): thank you all for lighting the torch, showing us the way and guiding us to a new way of thinking about finance

- Dent Global who helped us to shape and build our CLEARER™ model, in doing so we clarified the value within our services and understood how to share that value with our clients

- Justine, Andy and their production team at Really Bright Media for capturing the value we deliver on film

- Dave at Corbett Creative for his input on branding, design and digital marketing

- Tim, Ben, Dan and James at Albion Strategic Consulting who form our insourced investment committee and whose thinking and beliefs on how to set up and run an efficient and successful investment model run parallel with those views of our own. They have helped us to shape the exact model we deploy in its various weightings and without their input we would fall short of the mark

Thank you to all the (anonymised) clients who have featured in this book (and those who feature in our social media, brochure and websites) for letting us share their stories. The good we do is promoted to other families and, one way or another, we will end up making the difference we planned at the start to the 500 families we plan to reach.

Thank you to Michael Jacobson, Jimmie Joseph, Elliott Poole, Benjamin Fabi, Robert Wilcocks and Mark Clement for reading the penultimate final draft of my book from cover to cover. Your comments meant a lot and collectively had a positive impact on the end result.

Special thanks to my youngest brother Rob for being my wingman and for staying the course, particularly in the tough early years – and for giving me the best Christmas present I've ever received: *The Excellent Investment Advisor* by Nick Murray.[22] It even trumped the red Raleigh Grifter.

In a recent 'Wilcocks Clan' WhatsApp conversation with my parents and siblings, including my brother Rob, our mum Les asked, 'What about your book, Rob?'. Rob said he had 'outsourced it to Mart', jokingly suggesting I was a 'natural orator' – which of course I am not. This book has taken a mammoth or 'triple effort', as I put it in that conversation. I went on to say:

'that the main foundations underpinning what I talk about in the book have developed over the last eight years, in particular within our business, as a result of enhancements within our model that were put forward by ... Rob. So, you could say it exists as a result of us both. It just so happens that, over the last two years, with the support of the publisher Rethink Press, I've packaged up everything we do and bolted it into this book. So, it is very much a joint effort in that sense. And you can even go one step further and say it exists because of the three of us; had Mary [my sister] not spent ten hours a day working in the background with our clients, which I can assure you is a huge job, navigating everything that is necessary to run a £124 million asset book of business, I wouldn't have had the hour needed each day to knock it into shape.'

In fact, my partner Tahnee deserves equal merit because, frankly, as well as looking after our three children she also looks after me and creates space for me to be me, which is no mean feat. A small number of our clients have also arrived because of her: her attendance at the odd lunch here and there with clients adds a layer of gloss – every time. The truth is, she is as important as the rest of us for making it all tick. This work, and everything we are and do, exists due to the four of us.

The Author

Martin Wilcocks has been devoted to personal finance since joining Barclays Bank in 1989 aged 17. After a shaky start with undiagnosed dyslexia, grappling with data entry in machine rooms and struggling to balance tills after hours, he discovered a passion for 'talking to customers and helping them get what they want'.

Martin spent nine years in personal banking in Barclays branches throughout Liverpool, the Wirral and Chester before switching to Barclays Life as a financial adviser. He won several sales awards in his four years with Barclays Life, including Top New Adviser, then returned to Barclays Bank as a premier manager dealing with high-net-worth clients.

He became a financial adviser under the St. James's Place network umbrella in 2003, before setting up his own business in 2006. He was joined shortly after by his brother Rob and Wilcocks & Wilcocks have been working with clients throughout the UK ever since. Their CLEARER™ model encourages clients to plan for themselves and for the security of future generations, and they currently work with 115 families and 170 individual investors.

Martin is an award-winning top 1% wealth adviser featured in *The Times*, *The Telegraph* and *The Mail on Sunday*. He secured his professional qualifications at the Institute of Financial Services, APS Legal & Associates and The London Institute of Banking & Finance. He is a member of The Chartered Institute for Securities & Investment.

Read Martin's client testimonials at:

🌐 https://martinwilcocks.co.uk/testimonials

Lightning Source UK Ltd.
Milton Keynes UK
UKHW022229251122
412825UK00012B/630